MW01167563

THE PARABLES OF JESUS
AND THE PROBLEMS OF THE WORLD

The Parables of Jesus
and the Problems of the World

How Ancient Narratives Comprehend Modern Malaise

RICHARD Q. FORD

CASCADE *Books* · Eugene, Oregon

Cascade Books
An Imprint of Wipf and Stock Publishers
199 W. 8th Ave., Suite 3
Eugene, OR 97401

www.wipfandstock.com

paperback ISBN: 978-1-4982-3297-5
hardover ISBN: 978-1-4982-3299-9
ebook ISBN: 978-1-4982-3298-2

Cataloging-in-Publication data:

Names: Ford, Richard Q.

Title: The parables of Jesus and the problems of the world : how ancient narratives comprehend modern malaise / Richard Q. Ford.

Description: Eugene, OR : Cascade Books. | Includes bibliographical references.

Identifiers: ISBN: 978-1-4982-3297-5 (paperback) | ISBN: 978-1-4982-3299-9 (hardback) | ISBN: 978-1-4982-3298-2 (ebook).

Subjects: LCSH: Jesus Christ—Parables. | Title.

Classification: BT375.2 F67 2016 (print) | BT375.2 (ebook)

Manufactured in the USA

Quotations from the New Testament come from *New Revised Standard Version Bible (NRSV)*. Division of Christian Education of the National Council of the Churches of Christ in the United States of America, copyright ©1989.

Quotations from the Hebrew Bible or Old Testament come from *Tanakh: The Holy Scriptures: The New JPS Translation according to the Traditional Hebrew Text (NJPS)*. Philadelphia: Jewish Publication Society, copyright ©1985.

Quotations from the Gospel of Thomas come from *The Scholars Version (SV)*, Robert J. Miller, ed., *The Complete Gospels: Annotated Scholar's Version*. Revised and expanded edition. Sonoma, CA: Polebridge, 1994.

ABOUT THE COVER PHOTOGRAPH

The cover photograph is of a sculpture by Robert Taplin of New Haven, Connecticut, titled *Get Back! (The River Styx)*. (Used with permission.) The sculpture itself depicts a scene from Dante's *Inferno*. From left to right the characters are Phlegyas, the Boatman of Styx, Dante, Virgil, and, in the water, Pilippo Argenti, whom Dante variously describes as "loathsome" and "the maddog Florentine."

The relevant text from the *Inferno* reads as follows:

[Dante] ". . . who are you so fallen and so foul?"
And he [Argenti]: "I am one who weeps." And I then:
"May you weep and wail to all eternity,
for I know you, hell-dog, filthy as you are."
Then he stretched both hands to the boat, but warily
the Master shoved him back, crying, "Down! Down!
with the other dogs!"

Canto VIII, 35–41 (Trans. John Ciardi)

for

John Dominic Crossan

in admiration and appreciation

Contents

Acknowledgments | ix

Introduction | 1

1. Tenants and a Landlord, Iraq and the United States | 8

2. Slaves and a Master, the Sudan and China | 18

3. Jesus's Parable of the Talents: The Imaging and Mimicry of Empire | 29

4. Laborers and a Vineyard Owner, Iraqi Oil and the United States | 40

5. A Woman with Leaven, a Woman with a Jar, and A Man with a Sword: Gender Inequities | 52

6. A Slave and a Master, Main Street and Wall Street | 68

7. A Manager and a Rich Man, Afghanistan and the United States | 80

8. A Younger Son and a Father: Waiting for God's Restoring, or Restoring God's Waiting? | 94

9. The Poor and a Householder, The Third World and Debt | 106

10. A Widow and a Judge, Climate Change and Fossil Fuel Executives | 120

11. Summaries of This Book's Interpretations | 139

12. The Luring of Jesus and the Longing of God | 148

Appendix: Parable Boundaries | 163

Bibliography | 167

Acknowledgments

The author gratefully acknowledges permission to use the following previously published articles:

"Jesus' Parable of the Wicked Tenants and America's Invasion of Iraq." *The Fourth R* 20/5 (September–October 2007) 13–16. (Revised to form chapter 1.)

"Jesus' Parable of the Talents and the 2008 Olympics." *The Fourth R,* 21/4 (July–August) 2008, 13–15, 18–19, 24. (Revised to form chapter 2, with a segment placed in chapter 3.)

"Jesus' Parable of the Vineyard Workers and U.S. Policy on Iraqi Oil." *The Fourth R* 22/4 (July–August 2009) 3–6, 22 (Revised to form chapter 4.)

"Body Language: Jesus' Parables of the Woman with the Yeast, the Woman with the Jar, and the Man with the Sword." *Interpretation: A Journal of Bible and Theology* 56 (2002) 295–306. (chapter 5)

"Jesus' Parable of the Unforgiving Slave and the Wall Street Crisis of 2008." *The Fourth R* 24/3 (May–June 2011) 15–20, 22. (Revised to form chapter 6.)

"Jesus' Parable of the Dishonest Steward and America's War in Afghanistan." *The Fourth R* 25/3 (May–June 2012) 3–8. (Revised to form chapter 7.)

Introduction

JESUS INVITED HIS HEARERS "to enter the kingdom of God." This elusive metaphor might more aptly be translated "to enter the empire of God." For first-century Jewish sensibilities, an obvious allusion was to the crushing weight of imperial taxation enforced by the omnipresent military threat of Rome. How then can these images of "empire" and "God" possibly cohere? How then does one "enter" the empire of God?

This book proposes that the ways Jesus invites us to enter the empire of God are intimately embodied in the ways he invites us to enter his parables. Those listeners newly encountering his unfamiliar way of telling stories emerge from them in various states of uncertainty. Underlying their perplexity is Jesus's insistence that his hearers work to discover what he intended. He returns to us the taxing task of "entering." Hiding as well as revealing, his narratives offer unexpectedly difficult access to unexpectedly vibrant experience.

Focusing on eight of Jesus's longer parables and three of his shorter ones, this book explores ways to support readers as they attempt to expand the range and depth of their listening. It describes how awareness comes about not through ready access but only after extended seeking. Because their ironies are so exquisitely veiled, the profound effectiveness of these stories is easily blunted. Yet if listeners work to discern their possibilities, these narratives respond with impacts that surprise and awaken.

Locked within each of these eight stories are two parable characters—an overlord and an underling. Although separated by huge discrepancies in power, each needs the other. No one else is positioned to intervene. Their attempts at collaboration invariably collapse under the weight of inequality. The long-standing, unarticulated sequences undergirding these tragedies inform the analogues this book makes with modern distress. The capacity of these ancient stories to enfold such lengthy sequences becomes today's

1

resource for penetrating the deceptions so deeply embedded in contemporary global conflict.

What May Hinder Us From Sensing Possibility

Because they are unclear in what they are about, anyone who attempts to enter these parables must read understanding into them; perhaps their single most important attribute is their malleability. While we are constrained by the need to impose coherence, we are free to entertain a wide variety of options.

However, for many readers this range of options has become dangerously constricted. Because they have learned to focus on the blameworthy behavior of the parable's underling, readers have allowed its more powerful character to escape serious scrutiny. They have been persuaded by a widespread interpretive approach that sees in each parable's economically superior character, be he landlord, slave master, vineyard owner, rich man, or father, a figure for God. Given that dominant character's stance of self-confidence, this landowner, that master, this rich man, that father, then become endowed with the authority to reveal, from the top down, the parable's meaning.

Within such an interpretive framework, parable characters are from the outset divided into categories of black and white. On the one hand are those who are "all-good"—that is, commanding, authoritative, generous, and compassionate (the landowners, the slave masters, the rich man, the father). On the other hand are those who are "all bad"—that is, murderous, cowardly, unforgiving, envious, dishonest, profligate, and ungrateful (the tenants, the slaves, the laborers, the manager, the sons). If listeners discover in the superior character a figure for God, thus giving him not only all the respect but also all the work, they can then position themselves to have no work of their own to do. From such a vantage point, these narratives are no longer encountered as surprising or even puzzling.

However, would Jesus of Nazareth, focused as he was on discerning the desire of his God for *all* humankind, intend for his listeners to be drawn along such completely separate, walled-off paths, thereby protected from exploring the complexities that occur when humans interact across difference? Even more, would not Jesus's original peasant audiences (as do Third World peasants of our own era) have been extremely reluctant to promote precisely those who so abused them into representatives of their God?

In some quarters these multilayered stories are reduced to "simple stories for simple people." Such bias is encouraged and sustained by our Western economic privilege; only a modern Western sensibility would confuse illiteracy with lack of intelligence. The peasants of Jesus's era, schooled in the subtleties of torah storytelling, were almost certainly more attuned to the allusions lodged in Jesus's metaphors than are we post-Enlightenment "fact fundamentalists," who tend to assume that the shape of truth most often turns up consonant with the shape of fact.

It is astounding to realize how much a single prevalent assumption—that the dominant parable character somehow represents God—has dulled, muted, and ultimately drained away Jesus's profound but indirect critique of the unjust processes so endemic to the amassing of wealth. This book responds by scrutinizing the behavior of these dominant actors. It proposes that Jesus, while appearing to affirm their integrity, in fact subverts their authority. By working to recognize the superior's collusion in each parable's tragedy, readers enter novel sequences that move beyond the blameworthy behaviors of the underling and into the long-standing but disguised misconstructions imposed by the powerful. If we First World listeners can break free from perceiving as figures for God the necessarily violent participants in such exploitation, we may become more able to appreciate Jesus's extraordinary skill as he nonviolently engages us in challenging systemic injustice.

The Containing, Hiding, and Revealing of Violence

One strategy used in this book is to study sequence: that is, to focus on how the prior attitudes and actions of the overlord are profoundly implicated in each story's tragedy. At the level of content, these narratives are understood to have as their primary theme the unjust use of wealth and power. At the level of process, they may be seen as enclosing, exposing, and then muting the long-standing violence of the superior character. *Enclosing* comes as two persons separated by large differences in power are held together in a relationship of mutual dependency. *Exposing* comes first through the superior's unexamined controlling and then through the subordinate's distorted but easily blamed reactions. The *muting* of the overlord's violence occurs in three ways: (1) the superior exercises his power behind a facade of legitimacy, (2) the easily criticized responses of the underling distract listeners from examining the earlier exploiting behaviors of the overlord, and (3) the superior character steadfastly refuses to acknowledge the fact of his corrupt and corrupting dominance. (It is difficult to know which is harder to bear: the actual violence itself or the overlord's utter refusal to admit that what he is doing inflicts damage.)

Should readers begin to suspect the injustices inherent in the superior character's dominance, they can then become aware of how such a chronic misuse of power has infiltrated and undermined his blamed subordinate. While the conflicts in these stories originate in the superior's earlier coercion, their tragedies derive from the pervasive misunderstandings that grow over time when one person succeeds in dominating another. Across generations these misunderstanding deepen into what one writer has termed "permutations of tortured interdependence." From such a perspective these parables function as extraordinary commentaries on the malfunctioning hierarchies of power that chronically inhabit human institutions.

Jesus's understandings of money, debt, and control by the powerful are as cogent today as they were two thousand years ago. Grasping how parable participants were compromised by the political and economic realities in which they lived provides readers access to similar distorting forces at work in modern global conflict. By overcoming the temptation that Jesus himself seems to place in our way—that of simply blaming the underling—we can discover multiple analogues in our contemporary world. To illustrate such potential, this book interweaves these ancient narratives with carefully chosen, analogous contemporary issues: the war in Iraq, China in the Sudan, Iraqi oil, the recent financial crisis, the war in Afghanistan, nation-states' assumption of divinely ordained privilege, Third World debt, and the denial of climate change.

Some of these current issues will soon fade from awareness. For example, no one seems to mind any more that the recent war in Iraq was all about who profits from Iraq's oil. Once Americans stop dying, we turn away. Nonetheless, the attitudes of self-aggrandizement embedded in these events remain, recurring again and again in all their monotonously repetitive forms. For example, the greed of the talent master and his first two slaves, where increasing the wealth of a few inevitably means depleting the resources of many, remains as salient in 2009 CE as it did in 29 CE, just as evocative now as then of how the one percent still seeks to control the resources of the ninety-nine percent.

Represented in both ancient parable and contemporary analogue are the self-justifying initiatives of imperial power interacting with the

untoward reactions of those subjected to oppression. Readers may become uncomfortable with this strategy of correlation. As members of an
elite residing in the Western world, we may prefer not to ponder how our
dominance, like that of each parable's powerful character, is fundamentally
flawed. Our initial response to this idea is to be indignant. We immediately
say, "What have *we* done? We are good, freedom-loving people." Nonetheless it may be that we too, along with the parable's superior character, have
become unable to recognize both the ways in which we take advantage
of others and the ways in which others experience our domination. The
United States is an empire. Empires routinely take what belongs to others.
Empires are violent. We in America experience difficulty when trying to
recognize how often, in pursuit of the earth's resources, we have become the
perpetrators of violence. By engaging such analogues, we may be able to lay
hold of a countervailing, nonviolent power for change beckoning us from
deeply inside these ancient—and violent—narratives.

The Containing, Hiding, and Revealing of Nonviolence

Although they are containers of violence, these narratives function nonviolently. Their violence is lodged in their portrayal of the unacknowledged,
putatively normal structures of systemic injustice. Their nonviolence is
discovered in how they expose in deliberately subtle and disguised ways
this actual but denied violence. While these stories are built on the unequal
distribution and misuse of wealth (that is, on those economic and political
foundations in the ancient world that continue essentially unchanged into
our own time), they do not confront us directly with such hidden realities.
Rather, they require us to dig, to penetrate all the cover-ups, in order to
unearth the true sources of the needless hurt and useless destruction that
reside within their contours.

These stories do not impose; they beckon. They do not demand; they
lure. Readers are here introduced not only to the great complexity of Jesus's
parables but also to the great responsibility he entrusts to his listeners to
probe that complexity. We can then discover how these narratives may be
understood not as stories containing hidden messages to be deciphered but
rather as histories containing distorted sequences to be discerned.

Responding to the question, do I really want to spend my time with
this? this book encourages you to engage in a re-vision, in a looking again—
enhanced by sustained attention and bolstered by the promise that there is

more here, much more, than meets the eye. Having been stories with remarkable staying power for their time, they remain urgently needed stories
for our time. Across twenty centuries Jesus's parables still have the power to
expose the false promises in every effort to coerce, and the great dangers in
every temptation to control. Through their irony and subtlety, his parables
stand astride these commonplace entrances into human empire. They instead offer a distinctly different access to God's empire, to God's way of
ruling, to how God wants us to be with each other.

This book proposes that how we go about penetrating the distortions
confronting us in these parables has much to do with how, in their author's
imagination, we go about entering the kingdom of God. Presenting us with
painful tragedies, Jesus's parables have the potential to function as forums
in which we might suspect the hidden sources of these tragedies, reach for
greater equality across difference, and thereby step beyond them as carriers
of violence and into the kingdom of God.

If toward these imagined parable characters we embody the way God
relates to us and would have us relate to one another—not through coercion
but through allowing, not through controlling but through understanding—then these puzzling narratives will open up to us with an amazing
richness. By hearing these ancient stories juxtaposed with accounts of
modern malaise, we become better able to carve pathways through the
bramble thickets of contemporary economic and political dissembling that
so disguise the entrance to the kingdom—or intention or desire—of God.

TENANTS AND A LANDLORD

(The Wicked Tenants)

THE SITUATION

A man had a vineyard and leased it to tenant farmers and departed.

SCENE I

At harvest time he sent a slave to the tenant farmers to receive from them some of the produce of the vineyard. But they seized him and beat him and sent him away empty-handed.

SCENE II

He sent them another slave and they beat him too.

SCENE III

Then he sent his son to them, saying, "They will respect my son."
But the tenants said, "This is the heir,"
and they seized him and killed him.
    —Reconstruction by John S. Kloppenborg[1]

---

1. Versions of the Wicked Tenants appear in all three Synoptic Gospels as well as in the Gospel of Thomas (Mark 12:1b–8; Matt. 21:33b–39; Luke 20:9b–15; Thomas 65). The version cited here represents John S. Kloppenborg's scholarly "general approximation of the basic structure of the original parable." Kloppenborg, *Tenants*, 272 and n. 164. In his book's chapter 8, across some 58 pages, Kloppenborg justifies his reconstruction.

1

Tenants and a Landlord, Iraq and the United States[2]

Why would a father,
who possesses abundant evidence
that his distant tenant farmers violently oppose him,
propel his son into their midst unprotected?

JESUS'S PARABLES ARE EXCEEDINGLY brief. Even his longer parables, at least in the ways they were remembered, are far shorter than traditional short stories. Influenced by that brevity, we assume their time span to be equally brief. We thereby fail to suspect how much of "parable time" is entrusted to our imagining. By pushing backwards into the story—by asking, before this happened, what happened?—we can bring into focus a much longer sequence of events and thus position ourselves to discover how much the *entire* sequence matters.

Such potential is nowhere more available than in the parable of the Wicked Tenants. However, modern listeners have a hard time becoming aware of the history of exploitation that forms its foundation. The major reason for this difficulty is that Mark has transformed Jesus's story into an allegory, setting in stone its most popular interpretation. By drawing our

2. This chapter was first published in *The Fourth R,* 20,5 (Sept.–Oct. 2007) 13–16. Used with permission. Here I am particularly indebted to the work of Herzog, *Subversive Speech,* chap. 6.

attention to the simple task of breaking the allegory's code, he has diverted us from the far more difficult work of grasping the story's realities.

Having placed his presumably oft-spoken narrative on Jesus's lips during his passion-week confrontation with the Jerusalem temple authorities, Mark restricts its intended audience to an elite group. He then makes his own understanding clear. God is the vineyard owner, the vineyard is Israel, the slaves are the prophets, and the withholding tenants are those leaders of Israel who, having failed to provide justice, are now about to kill God's son. Having created his gospel perhaps four decades after Jesus's crucifixion, during the traumatic years immediately following the Roman destruction of Jerusalem, Mark imagines Jesus to be expecting that God "will come and destroy the tenants" (Mark 12:9). With profound irony (and against his own larger purposes), Mark thus wrests this ambiguous parable away from the imagination of a supremely nonviolent Jesus and returns it to him—at the very moment he is most determined to accept death rather than fight— as if it were an imperial sword.

Ambiguities Surrounding Our War in Iraq

One way to raise awareness of this story's ambiguities is to bring them into dialogue with the ambiguities surrounding what has arguably been one of the most perplexing political questions of the first decade of this century. Why did a handful of planners, at least seven months *before* 9/11/, decide to invade Iraq?[3]

---

3. Pulitzer Prize-winning author Ron Suskind gives a summary of then-Secretary of the Treasury Paul O'Neill's account of the aftermath of a meeting of the National Security Council, of which O'Neill was a member, held soon after the inauguration of President George W. Bush (and seven months before 9/11). "Beneath the surface was a battle O'Neill had seen brewing since the NSC meeting of January 30, [2001]. It was [Secretary of State Colin] Powell and his moderates at the state Department versus hard-liners like [Secretary of Defense Donald] Rumsfeld, [Vice President Dick] Cheney, and [Deputy Secretary of Defense Paul] Wolfowitz, *who were already planning* the next war in Iraq and the shape of a post-Saddam country. Documents were being prepared by the Defense Intelligence Agency, Rumsfeld's intelligence arm, mapping Iraq's oil fields and exploration areas and listing companies that might be interested in leveraging the precious asset." Suskind, *Price of Loyalty,* 96 (italics added). See also Mayer, "Contact Sport," who gained access to a top-secret document dated February 3, 2001, in which a high-ranking official of the National Security Council directed the NSC staff to cooperate with the National Energy Policy Development Group (headed by Vice President Dick Cheney) in assessing the military implications of the administration's energy plan. According to Mayer, the document envisioned the "melding" of two White House priorities: stepped-up pressure

Among a long list of reasons for the war, only the first two have retained enough currency to continue being promulgated. The rest have either fallen silent or never been acknowledged:[4]

1) to destroy Saddam Hussein

2) to create a new Middle East by projecting into it Western forms of democracy

3) to destroy Hussein's weapons of mass destruction

4) to undermine Hussein's support of al-Qaeda

5) to display to the post-Soviet world the invincibility of American military might

6) to secure bases from which to project American power

7) to preempt terrorists' ability to strike at American targets

8) to crush Israel's enemies

9) to provide chosen corporations with huge profits

10) to gain control over ten percent of the world's remaining oil

Following Hussein's death, this second justification for the war (that we have been generously engaged in spreading democracy) is the one that has remained most salient; it is also the one whose seeming beneficence and disowned self-interest resonates well with Jesus's parable.

Ambiguities Lodged in the Parable

The parable offers listeners an exceedingly puzzling question: Why would a father who possesses abundant evidence that his distant tenant farmers violently oppose him propel his son into their midst unprotected? If this question seems difficult to entertain, here is a contemporary, equally difficult question. Why would American leaders, fully informed about the centuries-old strife in Iraq among Kurds, Sunni Muslims, and Shia Muslims, send our troops into that ongoing conflict (about to be no longer held in check by a ruthless dictator) seriously undermanned?[5] I will argue that

on "rogue states" such as Iraq, and "actions regarding the capture of new and existing oil and gas fields." Cited in Klare, *Blood and Oil*, 70.

4. Most of these reasons are taken from Kinzer, *Overthrow*, 291–93.

5. A month before the U.S. invasion of Iraq (which began on March 20, 2003), the

the parable functions ambiguously, powerfully, and tragically essentially because the vineyard owner, throughout the entire time he dispatches unarmed envoys into the hands of manifestly violent peasants, persists in believing that his enterprise is lawful.

Exploitation, Then and Now

The absentee landlord in Jesus's story is a wealthy man. He has the capital to invest in a time-delayed luxury crop (grapes, for wine), something far beyond the means of the heavily taxed, subsistence-oriented peasantry. While he personally may have acquired his land fairly, he nonetheless represents a class of persons who have systematically stolen the land of smallholding peasants.

The Galilee of Jesus's time was an agrarian economy where perhaps 2 percent of the population controlled 50 percent of the wealth. Those at the top employed a two-step strategy to achieve such dominance. First, although they had lost their autonomy in subservience to Rome, they bought the right to levy the required tribute. Second, taxing the peasantry to the limit, they used their share of the exorbitant profits to make loans back to these same impoverished farmers, waiting only for the inevitable defaults before taking their land. Time and again, peasant smallholders were forced off their ancestral lands and left with no choice other than to become tenant farmers. Having reduced the peasantry to retaining only a fraction of their production, the aristocracy made off with both their property and its profit.[6]

Compare such ancient land grabbing with the following modern-day resource grabbing. In Iran in 1951, the democratically elected prime minister, Muhammad Mussadegh, a man *Time* magazine called "the Iranian George Washington," nationalized his country's oil industry. In response, John Foster Dulles, President Eisenhower's secretary of state, authorized

---

Chairman of the Joint Chiefs of Staff General Eric Shinseki told the Senate Armed Services Committee that "something in the order of several hundred thousand soldiers" would probably be required for postwar Iraq. This estimate was far higher than the figure being proposed (of one hundred thousand troops) by Secretary of Defense Donald Rumsfeld, and Rumsfeld rejected his Chairman's estimate in strong language (Schmitt, "Pentagon Contradicts General on Iraq Occupation Forces' Size"). As events later demonstrated, Rumsfeld, like the vineyard owner, was dead wrong.

6. For references in the literature supporting the assertions in this paragraph, see chapter 3. See also Kloppenborg, *Tenants,* 284–308.

the CIA to topple Mussadegh and bring to power Muhammad Reza Shah. In exchange for supporting twenty-five years of the Shah's enormously repressive rule, the U.S. gained control of Iranian oil. However, by exercising its assumed right to take over the resources of others (under the guise of fighting Communism), the U.S. forfeited a major opportunity to foster democracy, helped create the conditions that led to the Iranian Revolution of 1979, and contributed to that country's enduring resentment of the United States.[7]

As do members of the economically dominant class of any era, the vineyard owner has all his life participated in a process designed to transform prior injustice into seeming justice. The greed rampant among his fellows (and still obvious to the underclass) has gradually been domesticated. By the time of the parable this greed reappears translated into legalized normalcy. Thus the vineyard owner, who lives within the laws of his time (laws long ago decided upon by his fellow aristocrats), honestly believes he is worthy of respect. "This vineyard," he says, "is my lawful property. Since I have leased it to these tenant farmers, I have the right to my [lion's] share of its produce. Such arrangements are good for everyone; I benefit, and so do these landless peasants." He calculates that if only he could find a way to get them to recognize his authority, these tenant farmers would assuredly accept his claims.

Stephen Kinzer, a veteran *New York Times* foreign correspondent, writes:

> For more than a century, Americans have believed they deserve access to markets and resources in other countries. When they are denied that access, they take what they want by force, deposing governments that stand in their way. Great powers have done this since time immemorial. What distinguishes Americans from citizens of past empires is their eagerness to persuade themselves that they are acting out of humanitarian motives . . . They are hardly the first people to believe themselves favored by Providence, but they are the only ones in modern history who are convinced that by bringing their political and economic system to others, they are doing God's work . . . Generations of American leaders have realized that they can easily win popular support for their overseas adventures if they present them as motivated by benevolence, self-sacrificing charity, and a noble desire to liberate the oppressed.[8]

7. For a compelling description of these events, see Kinzer. *All the Shah's Men*.
8. Kinzer, *Overthrow*, 316, 315.

Kinzer's analysis, suggesting that we may be acting in the same way as the vineyard owner, may be difficult to hear. But if the vineyard owner uses his social and economic privilege to prevent himself from seeing how others see him, leading to tragic consequences, might we not be wise to reengage this parable in order to take a hard look both at ourselves and at our national interests—and to better understand how *we* are seen by others?

Who Perceives the Exploitation?

With remarkable skill Jesus creates within his parable two vastly differing perspectives, ones that coexist but never touch: that of the vineyard owner, who possesses both economic advantage and legal right, and that of the dispossessed farmers, who control only the worth of their labor. Neither can get the other to change. Variations in how listeners understand the parable depend largely on whether they struggle with the perspective of the overlord, the underling, or both.

The tenants have no prospect of repossessing their land, no hope of enjoying the fruits of their labor; they are permanently destined to work on behalf of those who took what was theirs. While the manner in which they lost control of their ancient heritage was legal, the tenants might be excused for thinking it unfair. However, given the great gap in power between themselves and their lord, they cannot speak in open protest. They are instead reduced to choking out their rage through an inarticulate pounding on the bodies of hapless messengers. Amazingly, the vineyard owner fails to suspect the depth of the anger exposed in these dishonoring attacks.

In this reading, it is precisely because he so completely embraces the long-standing aristocratic transformation of greed into lawfulness, supported by the ways in which he has blocked himself from learning how his tenants actually perceive him, that the vineyard owner is able to make such an egregious misjudgment. He assumes that the solution to his problem is only a matter of getting his tenants to recognize his authority; once they do so, he is certain they will respect his claims. He is tragically mistaken. His tenants know perfectly well who he is; they have long ago judged him to be an exploiter. However, the owner cannot allow such a perception of himself into his awareness. His calculations concerning how his dispossessed tenants will respond succeed only because he excludes data. He continues to exclude data as he propels his son, with no protection at all, into the grasp of obviously violent rebels.

With our invasion of Iraq, the tragedy of Jesus's parable leaps into our midst. We too had confidence that our intentions would be met with respect and that in the course of protecting ourselves we would be seen as freeing an oppressed nation. However, just as in the parable the son's innocence had no effect on the tenants' hostility, so in Iraq our soldiers' good intentions had no effect on the insurgents' outrage. "'There was never any buildup of intelligence that says it [the insurgency] is coming, it's coming, it's coming, this is the end you should prepare for,' General Tommy Franks said later. 'It did not happen, never saw it. It was never offered.'"[9] Those who planned the invasion, and we who followed them into it, anticipated neither the insurgency nor the ensuing civil war. Instead they and we believed that Iraqi people would welcome us as liberators—and then set about establishing a stable democracy.[10]

How Do We Listen?

Bernard Brandon Scott, a leading expert on the parables, underscores how this narrative "points out the horror and hopelessness of the situation. To reclaim the inheritance by violence will lead only to an unending cycle of violence."[11] Scott is here attuned to how the parable draws listeners forward to imagine a destructiveness that propels itself onward long after the story ends.

However, is not access to the *source* of this interminable sequence of violence found disguised inside the vineyard owner's certainty that his tenants will in fact respect his claims? Listeners can use this certainty to probe

9. The *New York Times*, Oct. 20, 2004, quoted in Kinzer, *Overthrow*, 314. Army General Tommy Franks was the military commander who led the invasion of Iraq. General Franks' mission, according to then President George W. Bush, was "to disarm Iraq of weapons of mass destruction, to end Saddam Hussein's support for terrorism, and to free the Iraqi people" ("President's Radio Address, March 22, 2003").

10. From its inception under British rule, Iraq has been a state without internal cohesion. Profound fault lines crisscross its body politic. Embedded within all three of its mutually antagonistic subgroups (Kurd, Sunni Muslim, and Shia Muslim) is a split between desert (or mountain) tribal cultures and the contrasting religious and secular values found among the educated urban middle class. (See, for example, Mackey, *Reckoning*, especially chapter 2.) More important, Arab culture in general has experienced neither a Renaissance nor a Reformation nor an Enlightenment—foundations that Europe (and later the United States) required in order to build, across five centuries, Western democratic institutions.

11. Scott. "On the Road Again," 15.

back beyond the beginning of the story, discovering how the violence first originated inside the owner's aristocratic class; discerning how it was then disowned both by the owner and his aristocratic colleagues; and finally understanding how it was re-created inside the tenants, hiding in wait until it exploded back upon the owner. Reflection on such a convoluted sequence can lead to an awareness of the parable's tragic irony. By needing so much to imagine himself conforming to law and therefore worthy of respect, the owner actively participates in destroying the person he most loves.

Evidence both of Jesus's genius and of his noncoercive teaching style may be found in how completely he entrusts to his listeners the work of deciding how far back into his parable to probe and how much of its disguise to penetrate. It is as if Jesus knows he cannot tell us who we are but can only lure those willing to go there into the uncomfortable position of suspecting.

Have we, like the vineyard owner, convinced ourselves that our intentions are lawful and our purposes welcome? Have we, like him, remained ignorant of how these intentions play out among those who see us, because we consume far too large a share of the earth's resources, as exploiters? Only after the parable ends, when news of his son's murder eventually reaches him, will this father, in a brutal flash of illumination, confront the enormity of his error. Does not Jesus here give us resources whereby we might better understand the sources of our own (still not abundantly clear) miscalculations?

SLAVES AND A MASTER
(The Talents)

THE SITUATION

For it is as if a man, going on a journey, summoned his slaves[1]

SCENE I

and entrusted his property to them; to one he gave five talents, to another two, to another one, to each according to his ability. Then he went away.

SCENE II

The one who had received the five talents went off at once and traded[2] with them, and made five more talents. In the same way, the one who had the two talents made two more talents. But the one who had received the one talent went off and dug a hole in the ground and hid his master's money.

SCENE III

After a long time the master of those slaves came and settled accounts with them. Then the one who had received the five talents came forward, bringing five more talents, saying "Master, you handed over to me five talents; see, I have made five more talents." His master said to him, "Well done, good and trust-worthy slave; you have been trustworthy in a few things, I will put you in charge of many things . . ." And the one with the two talents also came forward saying, "Master, you handed over to me two talents; see, I have made two more talents." His master said to him, "Well done, good and trustworthy slave; you have been trustworthy in a few things. I will put you in charge of many things . . ."

Then the one who had received the one talent also came forward, saying, "Master, I knew that you were a harsh man, reaping where you did not sow; and gathering where you did not scatter seed, so I was afraid, and I went and hid your talent in the ground. Here you have what is yours." But his master replied, "You wicked and lazy slave! You knew, did you, that I reap where I did not sow, and gather where I did not scatter? Then you ought to have invested my money with the bankers, and on my return I would have received what was my own with interest. So take the talent from him, and give it to the one with the ten talents" (Matthew 25:14–28 (NRSV).

1. For centuries nearly every English translation of the two slave parables in this book has rendered the Greek word *doulos* inaccurately as "servant." (This bias is less evident when *doulos* is encountered in the Pauline Epistles, where the word often receives its proper meaning of "slave.") "Servant" obscures the term's essential significance for these parables, namely, that one human be-ing retains complete control over the life choices of another. Such has been the strength of this bias that it took the translators of the august Revised Standard Version until 1989, in the New Revised Standard Version, to render the word *doulos* correctly as "slave."

2. "Traded" is a too precise and therefore misleading translation of the Greek verb *ergadzomai*, which means "to work" or "to be active."

2

Slaves and a Master, the Sudan and China[3]

Why would a slave, seemingly terrified of his master's recrimination, refuse to do what he knows his master wants?

HOPING TO IMPROVE THEIR image abroad, the leaders of China, on August 8, 2008, stepped onto the world stage as hosts of the Summer Olympics. In turn, Steven Spielberg, one of America's foremost living film directors, who agreed in March of 2007 to become an artistic consultant to the Games, might have done much to enhance the opening and closing Olympic ceremonies. Over a billion television viewers worldwide were to have front-row seats for this premier example of Chinese-American collaboration. But such collaboration was not to be.

This Chinese-American moment takes place against a background of long-standing tragedy. Across the world in Darfur, at least four hundred thousand Sudanese have been killed, between 80 and 90 percent of black-African villages destroyed, millions displaced, and thousands upon thousands continue to die, some quickly and some slowly. Racism, the most ancient of prejudices, motivates this profound travesty. The Sudanese

3. This chapter was first published in *The Fourth R,* 21.4 (July–Aug., 2008) 13–15, 18–19, 24. Used with permission. For its basic orientation I am indebted to the seminal work of two authors: Ngũgĩ's *Devil on the Cross* and Herzog's "Vulnerability of the Whistle-blower," chapter 9 in *Subversive Speech.*

government is deliberately and viciously enabling Sudanese Arabs to occupy Sudanese black-African land.[4]

These two events—the Olympics in Beijing and the genocide in Darfur—appear disconnected; certainly the leaders in China hoped to keep their lack of concern for human rights in Darfur completely separate from their prestigious presentation of the Games. One way to bring together such seemingly detached fragments, including Steven Spielberg, into some kind of deeply troubling whole may be discovered, I believe, if we struggle to reintegrate the broken apart pieces lodged within our common misunderstanding of one of Jesus's most familiar parables.

Our Difficulty Seeing What Is Actually Going On

When we encounter Jesus's narrative of the Talents (Matt 25:14–28; partial parallel in Luke 19:13–24), we are quite sure we understand what is taking place. We see a wealthy man entrusting large sums of money[5] to his subordinates to invest; he leaves, returns, and then distributes praise or blame.

Following Matthew, we assume the master to be a figure for God or Christ, who will return after an absence to reward or reject his servants. We therefore imagine the master to be someone who has both the integrity and the intent to tell us what is actually going on.

Even though Jesus tells us several times what is in fact going on, we persist in misunderstanding. Present-day readers may have difficulty grasping the subtleties of how one goes about making large sums of money in southern Galilee in the early part of the first century, but Jesus leaves no doubt about the criminal nature of the master's enterprise; twice we are told that this man goes through life "reaping" where he did not "sow." He is a thief and a villain. (This depicting is as close as Jesus comes, anywhere on record, to describing the Roman Empire.)

---

4. Reeves, *Long Day's Dying*, 9, 10, 17. What the Arab Sudanese are doing to the African Sudanese is essentially no different than what European immigrants, later called Americans, did to native American peoples. Sudanese land grabbing may also be understood as a prescient example of climate-driven resource conflict; the drying up of neighboring Lake Chad is severely constricting available human habitat.

5. The "talent" in this parable was originally a measure of weight varying in size from about fifty-eight to eighty pounds. By New Testament times the silver talent had become a unit of money worth six thousand denarii. Assuming one denarius as a day's wage for a laborer, to earn a talent would take such a laborer, working every day, over twenty years.

What Is Actually Going On?

It is important to keep in mind the corrupt processes introduced in chapter 1 and explored in detail in chapter 3, by which this master and his slaves made all of their profits. In Jesus's time perhaps 2 percent of the population controlled 50 percent of the wealth. These elites built up their position in two stages. Purchasing the right to levy taxes, and backed up by the occupying Roman military, they first demanded the Galilean peasantry surrender a third of their annual harvest. None of this "tax" was returned in the form of any benefit. After passing on much of the extorted wealth to Rome, the elites still had substantial amounts to keep for themselves. The peasants had nothing left for protection against inevitable crop failure; one bad year and they were forced to borrow, and for collateral they had only their ancestral land. Flush with surpluses and eager to lend, the aristocrats had only to wait until the weaker among these already stressed farmers became unable to pay. Then the lenders foreclosed, took the land, and forced the previous owners to become tenant farmers. Given that this was the only way possible in that agrarian economy to make huge profits, this was how the master and his two slaves did it—and it was entirely legal.[6]

But it was not just. In a 1993 article on this parable, Richard L. Rohrbaugh pointed out the fact of limit in such a closed economy. "There simply is not enough of anything to go around or any way to increase the size of the pie . . . What this means is . . . a larger share for one automatically means a smaller share for someone else." Thus, " a master getting one thousand percent on his money [according to Luke 19:16] would be viewed as greedy to the core."[7] Christoph Kahler is more explicit; he sees the master as "inhumanly hard," "a blood-sucker," "an oppressor," and "a thief."[8]

6. For references supporting the assertions in this paragraph, see chapter 3.

7. Rohrbaugh, "Peasant Reading," 33, 35.

8. Kahler, *Jesu Gleichnesse*, 171, 172, 173. A large amount of work appears necessary, often in collaboration with people who are poor and dispossessed, to rediscover what was once a given. For two of the places where this insight first broke into American awareness, see Fortna, "Jesus' Parable of the Talents," 211–28. Here Fortna describes a prison inmate who, when describing the master, suddenly realizes, "He exploitin' me, man!" (214). See also Cardinal, *Gospel in Solentiname*, 4:42, quoted in Fortna, "Underclass Eyes," 215n8), where Nicaraguan *campesinos* tentatively perceive the third slave's courage: "The guy didn't get much, one talent; he didn't cooperate . . . He was conscientious, because he didn't have the strength to exploit his brothers and sisters." In a magnificent chapter, (*Subversive Speech,* chapter 9) Herzog built on these earlier insights to create a comprehensive interpretation. Referring to the work of Cardenal, Herzog (ibid., 160–61) writes that of "all the contemporary commentators on the parable, the peasants

In a novel based on this parable, written originally in Gikuyu and published in English in 1982, the Kenyan postcolonialist author Ngũgĩ wa Thiong'o engages the conceit of a white colonialist entrepreneur who is forced by African nationalists to flee; this man then entrusts both his capital and his tactics to retainer Africans, who in turn become subordinate but no less sophisticated exploiters. Ngũgĩ has the last retainer challenge the entire enterprise.

> You, lord and master, member of the white race, I have discov-
> ered your tricks! I have discovered your real name, Imperialist,
> that's your real name, and you are a cruel master. Why? Because
> you reap where you have never sown. You grab things over which
> you have never shed any sweat. You have appointed yourself the
> distributor of things which you have never helped to produce.
> Why? Just because you are the owner of capital. And so I went and
> buried your money in the ground to see if your money would yield
> anything without being fertilized by my sweat or that of any other
> man. Behold, here is your 100,000 shillings, exactly as you left it.[9]

The third slave in Jesus's parable openly accuses his master of taking what does not belong to him. In response the master never challenges
this description of himself—only his subordinate's refusal to conform to it.
Nonetheless, we in the West persist in trusting him; nearly all of modern
First World interpretation decides that this parable master, when accounting for his own and others' behavior, is an unbiased and accurate judge.

China, Sudan, and Oil

Imperial elites of every age routinely attribute unquestioned authority to
their own entitlement. Just as routinely they suppress any protest from peoples weaker than themselves. In this regard China as an emerging empire
behaves no differently than does the United States as an established one. In
order to take for themselves what belongs to others, both empires make al-
liances with corrupt governments at the expense of common citizens. However, in their efforts to win control over more of the earth's resources, the
Chinese are distinguished from the Americans in one important regard:
they are far less conflicted in their disdain for human rights.

---

of Solentiname were the ones to intuit the economic system that underlies the parable
[as] . . . 'a very ugly example . . . of exploitation.'"

9. Ngũgĩ, *Devil on the Cross*, 84–85.

Both because of security risks during Sudan's civil war and because of political differences between the U.S. and Sudanese governments, the American oil giant Chevron suspended its initially promising operations in Sudan in 1984 and left the country completely in 1992. One of its major successors, Talisman of Canada, pulled out in 2002, partly in response to pressure from human rights groups, who repeatedly pointed out the relationship between revenues paid by Talisman and the capacity of the otherwise impoverished Sudanese government to engage in military repression. Ironically, these pullouts created a vacuum into which others entered who were far less responsive to the issue of human rights.

With its own oil resources drying up, the China National Petroleum Corporation (CNPC) began investing in Sudanese oil fields in the late 1990s; its involvement has increased steadily ever since. Profits are not the primary objective; energy security is. In exchange China provides Khartoum with major sources of revenue, access to military arms, and international political protection. Without its income from oil, the heavily indebted Sudanese government could not possibly afford both the aircraft and the militias necessary to sustain its genocide in Darfur. However, unlike its Western counterparts, the CNPC, controlled almost entirely by the Chinese government, has remained impervious to accusations of human rights abuse.[10]

Steven Spielberg

In our example, oil is first sucked up by the Chinese government, with some of the profits remaindered to needed intermediaries (the government in Khartoum). In Jesus's parable, tax revenues are first sucked up by the slave master (a figure for Rome), with some of the profits remaindered to well-positioned slaves (figures for those Jewish aristocrats who thrived in subservience to Rome).

Within this morass of unfeeling greed we find, still waiting for us, the third slave. This man's designation as a slave is misleading; he was of a competence and standing sufficient to command the trust of an exceedingly wealthy and therefore most discerning aristocrat. However, by daring to describe how things really are, by becoming a whistle-blower, this man risks losing the only security he possesses—his lord's approval.

10. Information in the above two paragraphs is from Patey, *Complex Reality,* 14–16, 21–24, 32–34.

To highlight this third slave's dilemma and to grasp the depth of his courage, I turn to the contemporary example of Steven Spielberg. Given an estimated fortune of over three billion dollars, with innumerable awards, and wide recognition as one of Hollywood's foremost living film directors, Spielberg's fame and power present an apt analogue to the prestige and ability of the parable's third slave.

Even more useful for our analogy is Spielberg's agreement in March of 2007 to become an artistic consultant to the 2008 Olympic ceremonies. His decision placed him in a dilemma similar to that of the third slave: either collaborate with powerful oppressors or resign. In his statement announcing his decision to withdraw, he wrote, "At this point my time and energy must be spent not on Olympic ceremonies but on doing all I can to help bring an end to the unspeakable crimes against humanity that continue to be committed in Darfur."[11] (Spielberg faced considerably less risk than the third slave, both by his citizenship and by his reputation. The former possessed neither. The third slave's dangerous exposure instead resonates more closely with that of another parable character: the courageous widow of chapter 10.)

Criticism flowed in, citing Spielberg's unwarranted intrusion and arrogance. But most daunting was the challenge that his action would simply prove ineffective. Realists readily termed quixotic any effort by individual celebrities to protest China's support of Khartoum's genocide. They pointed to what happened in 1999 when the Clinton administration, partly in response to human rights advocates, blocked the China National Petrolium Corporation from accessing the immense capital offerings of American financial markets. Although the CNPC's inability to list shares on the New York Stock Exchange wound up costing them an estimated twelve billion dollars, China put no pressure on Khartoum; their overriding need for energy security trumped this significant attempt by the United States to secure human rights.[12]

However, others have argued that on the occasion of China's hosting the Olympics, with the eyes of the world upon them, even such a modest

11. Milmo et al, "In Olympic Year."

12. Patey, *State Rules*, 14. The emerging Chinese empire is behaving no differently than has every empire throughout recorded history, including our own. The elites of empire suck up as much of the available wealth as they can. However, the Chinese are given to economic, not military, imperialism. Employing the vast wealth they have earned, largely from us, they are using it without firing a shot to secure a lion's share of the earth's remaining resources. See, for example, Moyo. *Winner Take All.*

threat to their prestige might have some influence. While the Chinese leadership would never tolerate interference in the political oppression of their own people, they could conceivably be persuaded, through concern that their image might be tarnished, at least to reduce their interference with the infusion into Darfur of a robust United Nations peacekeeping force. In any event, if Spielberg's protest in fact had some impact, no one outside of a few Chinese leaders would know, and none would acknowledge. (That nonviolent protest does not coerce recognition of its effectiveness is partly what makes it effective.)

The Third Slave

> *Master, I knew that you were a harsh man, reaping where you did not sow, and gathering where you did not scatter seed; so I was afraid, and I went and hid your talent in the ground. Here you have what is yours.*

Coming forward to account for his behavior, the third slave appears confused. However, looked at more closely, his speech holds together a stunning contradiction. After telling his master how afraid he is of him, the slave proceeds to inform him that he did not do what he knew his master wanted. He never acknowledges, either by showing anxiety or offering remorse, that these two attitudes of submission and disobedience do not cohere.

The master has preceded his subordinate in imposing his own contradiction and his own denial. To his slave he says, "I want you to act as an exploiting master, and yet I want you to behave as a subservient slave; I do not even now acknowledge the conflict in what I am saying." The master, in this matter of aristocratic control, has obligations of his own he has yet to embrace. Considerable irony resides in the last slave's description of the master's character. "You are a harsh man," he observes. "You reap where you did not sow"—that is, you receive in my seeming lack of initiative a disappointment shaped by your own failure to recognize the endless conflict residing within your pervasive domination of everyone around you.

The last slave could hardly have found a more effective way to offend this particular master; no option available to him was better calculated to incur the displeasure of such an intensely aggrandizing aristocrat than doing nothing at all. By burying the money, the slave counters every effort of his lord to corrupt him. By refusing to take advantage of others, he knowingly provokes his superior's rage. By rejecting the exploiter's offer to become a subordinate exploiter, he risks losing everything.

The slave's indirectness is at the center of the parable's ambiguity. One can only admire the man's deft touch. For his resistance to be effective, the slave must leave his master uncertain whether the hit he has received has been intended. Should the slave register his protest with anything even slightly more obvious, he would provoke, instead of disappointment and puzzled anger, only a smoothly rationalized scorn—followed, of course, by retaliation. His indirectness gives this subordinate not only his best chance to register his voice but also his best chance to survive.

In this reading the third slave is superbly calculating. Within the constraints of his position, he is engaged in a skillfully disguised attack upon his lord's presumption. Under cover of a cowering facade, he has in fact undertaken a calculated rejection. Citing fear as his motive, he is refusing to exploit. He will resist imposing on others what has been perpetrated upon himself. It is as if the slave is saying, with a carefully crafted slyness, "I will be hard on a hard man by being soft."

Here one might conceive of a struggle between equals distorted by inequality. When the test comes, the slave neither exploits nor steals; instead, he buries. His seeming passivity is, of course, a dangerous activity. By doing nothing at all, he engages in a courageous effort to maintain his integrity. Pressed by his subordinate's disguised resistance, the master explodes in anger. But the more he complains, the more his hypocrisy is revealed. "Deprive this man," he says, "who has dared to deprive *me*—but never mind how, all of my life, I have tried to deprive everyone I can." Nonetheless, the master is sincerely convinced of his hurt. Along with generations of his class before him, he long ago seduced himself into believing that he has the right to appropriate the resources of others. His rage is evidence of his conviction.

Could it be that this parable is evoking with great sensitivity the difficult position of a conflicted member of the Jewish retainer class struggling to hold on to authenticity while immersed in the compromises endemic to his class? Could it be that the last slave's seeming timidity rather represents one person's courageous efforts to retain his ethical footing? If so, one arrives at a place of wonder; how can anyone move in such narrow straits? On the one hand are demands for conformity widespread in a retainer class thoroughly overtaken by corruption and motivated by greed. On the other hand are this person's still-alive yearnings for integrity. The parable may be capturing his painful dilemma. For the only way out of his slavish mimicry of Rome, the only way back to his Jewish heritage of justice, is to refuse the opportunities of his privileged enslavement. But to reject the exploiter's proffered role of subordinate exploiter, to disdain the opportunity to imitate, is to provoke anxious ridicule, enraged censure, and eventual ostracism. In the end, this seemingly incompetent and cowardly third slave, this underling so familiar with both controlling and being controlled, emerges as one of the great unsung heroes of the Bible.

How Do We Listen?

Many of Jesus's longer parables (e.g., the Wicked Tenants, the Talents, the Vineyard Workers, the Unforgiving Slave, the Dishonest Steward, and the Prodigal Son) involve the entrusting of money or property across gaps of inequality. The breakdown in trust endemic to such inequality renders these stories extraordinary descriptions of how powerful elites, perpetrating larger systemic injustice under the guise of law, break apart the fragile integrity of those subjected to exploitation and thereby, without being held accountable, deepen the tragic fissures in human relatedness.

In this reading Jesus is addressing not so much his deprived fellow peasants as those members of the Jewish retainer class still able to struggle with the anomalies inherent in profiting through their enslavement to pagan power. Given their Jewish heritage of justice, some of these retainers might still be susceptible to perceiving both the corruptness of the master and the courage of the seemingly cringing third slave. From these possibilities it is not such a great leap to suppose that we American Christians may first of all be characterized, alongside such collaborators, as "slaves." From such a position, are we not here lured to join the third slave in challenging to the best of our ability the established order of exploitation?

Here we come upon a truly remarkable aspect of how Jesus told his stories. While directly describing both the hardened realities of imperial power and the serious costs of mounting any challenge, he does not corner his audience. He does not announce what to do. He does not force confrontation. Rather, he disguises, allows, and beckons. Jesus twice tells his listeners that the master is a criminal. But then he so skillfully enhances aristocratic authority that many hearers are pulled to imbue this same criminal with integrity.

Here Jesus imposes on his listeners a similar pressure to surrender and conform that the master imposes on these slaves. Within the tangled brambles of the master's controlling, Jesus appears to be hiding the way into the kingdom of God, into God's intent for humanity. Could it be that he so passionately wants our embracing of God's desire to be by effortful choice that he makes his hearers work so hard to find the way? Or could it be that he is here representing the *only* way in?

For those ready to push past this nearly seamless imitation of oppression, Jesus invites his listeners to engage the complexities of the third slave's position. Should he submit to his master's demand? What about justice? Should he protest his master's greed? What about his own security? To those ready to entertain the tensions inherent in this more complicated realm, Jesus then provides such listeners with freedom to range among options. Is this third slave, because he is by character conservative and careful, altogether convinced that his single task is to keep the money safe? Or, having been a slave all his life, is he so unprepared for independent initiative that he is overwhelmed and stops functioning? Or, within the severe constraints of his position, is he engaged in a superbly calculated protest against his lord's presumption? Listeners may find what they will. But to be open to this last option, they must leave off concentrating simply on the slave's character and turn to engage the master's impinging entitlement.

Listeners who choose this last pathway then encounter in the third slave a challenge to power that appears worse than useless. But is it so? Aided by the third slave, is Jesus offering us the chance to reestablish that essential link, so often denied, between our exploiting and the suffering of others? Such imagining is difficult for us in the First World. Being so completely cut off from those whom our economic priorities oppress, we are prevented from feeling how our gains cause others' loss.

Any awakened empathy on our part, however, may bring us closer to the ways Jesus embodies his understanding of God's desire: first, as longing for all to share equally in what the earth provides; second, as yearning for us to make it so; and third, as fully aware of the costs to us should we attempt to establish such equality. In this reading, for this parable, Jesus is portraying God as standing alongside this courageous and condemned third slave—while we continue to revile him. What if, instead, we contemplate changing sides? Caught in our dilemma, we may yet discern, emerging in close proximity to the third slave's risk-filled opposition, another seemingly futile challenge to power: Jesus's own defiance during the final days of his life inside the courtyards of the Jerusalem temple.

3

Jesus's Parable of the Talents:
The Imaging and Mimicry of Empire

IN RELATION TO OUR own global society so deeply scarred by the unequal distribution of wealth, the previous chapter sought to demonstrate the immediacy of Jesus's parable of the Talents. The present chapter pauses in this attempt at contemporary relevance in order to demonstrate further the remarkable ways this narrative embodies the very imperial structures it so deftly challenges. A more ready appreciation of Jesus's superb artistry in this instance requires an overview of the historical research documenting these same imperial structures so endlessly familiar to his original listeners. Some readers may choose to bypass this excursion into the parable's form and into the scholarly literature; others may find it of value.

Because aristocrats so completely controlled the production of classical literature, few peasant descriptions of ancient imperialism survive. As a metaphor for the agrarian empire of Rome, this parable is one of those few. Astonishingly, it both images and then mimics the very imperialist structures it subverts.

The parable images empire by evoking its polarities and thereby framing its vacant middle, namely, the absence of any law able to intervene. "Master" and "slavish subordinates" accurately capture the two complementary groupings essential for effecting the imperial transfer of wealth from the control of the many to the control of the few. At empire's narrow and articulate apex are found the exploiting slave master together with his well-appointed slaves; these represent both the Roman overlords and the Jewish aristocracy (together with the needed retainer class of bureaucracy and military). At its inarticulate base (and therefore implied but not represented in the parable itself) is the mass of exploited peasants required to create the expropriated wealth. The aristocracy justifies its dominance by imposing self-serving rationalizations into those unable to fight back. To maintain their artificially constructed belief-system, the oppressors work endlessly to silence the oppressed. The stronger steadfastly press their versions of reality into the weaker and then with equal tenacity resist experiencing or even acknowledging the painful consequences of what they themselves have imposed.

The parable then mimics precisely this aristocratic imposition of its own self-aggrandizing, self-justifying "reality." The master's uncritical description of his personal behavior stands as an unchallenged summary of imperial ideology. "I reap," he says, "where I did not sow, and I gather where I did not scatter" (Matt 25:26). While the parable's context is one of purported law, it in fact represents lawlessness. Every definition of what is lawful is controlled by the slave master; without opposition, he asserts the lawless conviction lodged within the aristocratic minority that they are in fact entitled to whatever they can take from the vast majority.[1]

As in empire itself, so in the parable all other alternatives are ruthlessly excluded. Within the narrative no law challenges the aristocracy's predatory stance, and no voice is permitted to resurrect such law. Crucial to the parable's functioning and to the economic model on which it is based is the absence of any middle term capable of curtailing the aristocracy's lawless abuse.

In this absent middle is situated the third slave. As an exploited member of the retainer class, he is called upon by his master to exploit. Because he lacks the support of independent lawgivers, this third slave's refusal, exceedingly dangerous, is by necessity both constricted and disguised. Appearing inept, he is hiding behind a facade of cowardliness in order to effect a covert opposition.

---

1. The saying appended at the parable's end, so perplexing to Christian piety, stands as a second summation of this aristocrat's definition of reality, a summation that again represents in condensed form the central reality of empire: "For to all those who have, more will be given, and they will have an abundance; but from those who have nothing, even what they have will be taken away" (Matt 25:29, NRSV); see Hanson and Oakman, *Palestine*, 118. For a contemporary analogue documenting how the American middle class has been systematically impoverished in favor of a new ruling elite, see Bartlett and Steele, *Betrayal*.

The parable then proceeds to immerse its listeners in a version of the third slave's deception and risk, behaviors necessarily distorted by empire's prior coercions. Listeners must work hard first to suppose, then to probe, and finally to identify the actual sources of this subordinate's disguised behaviors; they are thereby invited to suspect and then to track, but only if they determine to do so, the covered-over and nearly hidden footsteps of this seemingly uncertain yet strikingly courageous resistor.

The Master

First-century Palestine was part of the increasingly commercialized and monetized agrarian empire of Rome. Agrarian empire of any era may be conceptualized as a complementary hierarchy of exploiters and exploited. Within an enclosed, misshapen pyramid, resources are systematically sucked up from the enlarged base to engorge the minuscule apex. Gerhard Lenski writes, "On the basis of available data, it appears that the governing classes of agrarian societies" ["rarely contain{ing} . . . more than 2 per cent of the population"²] "probably received at least a quarter of the national income of most agrarian states, and that the governing class and ruler together usually received not less than half."³

Lenski adds, "To fully understand how these vast accumulations of wealth came into existence, one must take into account *the proprietary theory of the state* which dominated the thinking of most men of power in virtually all agrarian societies. According to this theory, the state is a piece of property which its owner may use, within broad and somewhat ill-defined limits, for his personal advantage." Lenski then observes, "property consists of rights, not of things, particularly of rights to things which are in short supply."⁴

The minuscule governing class of the Roman Empire relentlessly extracted wealth from its vast pool of laborers. Through innumerable patronage webs these overlords collected and then redistributed that wealth first among themselves and then to the small surrounding retainer class of bureaucrats, landowners, and soldiers. The orientation of these ruling groups was hierarchical, authoritarian, exploitative, and punitive.⁵

2. Lenski, *Power and Privilege*, 219.

3. Ibid., 228, cited by Crossan, *Historical Jesus*, 45.

4. Ibid., 218.

5. See Carney, *Shape of the Past*, 63, 90, 92–94, 101, 171, 250, and 337, partly cited by

Martin Goodman makes much of the possibility that a primary cause within Judea for the first Jewish revolt against Rome (66–73 CE) was this relentless aristocratic aggrandizing of wealth.[6] Goodman describes the two complementary methods employed by the aristocracy for this purpose of reaping where they had not sown. The first was taxation and then, with the peasantry thereby deprived of any savings, the second was land expropriation. The latter was accomplished through high-interest loans and was sustained by the promulgation of the *prosbul* measure. Because of the natural vagaries of agricultural production, what followed were inevitable foreclosures.[7]

The overall view that in Palestine during the Herodian period the elites coerced an increasing peasant alienation from the land seems to be widely accepted. Fiensy, for example, summarizes his 1991 book on the subject as follows:

> Throughout the following chapters runs a common thread: the effect of changing land tenure on the lives of the peasant class. We begin the investigation by describing the land-tenure ideal in Palestinian society. Next we summarize the changes in land tenure brought about by the Hellenistic and Roman Periods, namely, the growth of the large estates. We then detail the effect of these changes on the economic standard of living of the peasant.[8]

Fiensy goes on to document a steady lowering in that peasant standard of living imposed by aristocratic expropriation of peasant land.[9] This overall position is in line with the earlier work of Applebaum.[10]

Crossan, *Historical Jesus*, 59.

6. M. Goodman, "First Jewish Revolt," 417–27.

7. See Hanson and Oakman, *Palestine*, 142: "The *prosbul* measure, attributed to Hillel (actually originating in Helenistic-Egyptian law), evaded the prescription of Deut. 15:1–2 [preventing, through remission of debts every seven years, the irrevocable alienation of land ownership] and permanently turned the debtor over to the creditor through the agency of the courts . . . [T]he debtor could then be evicted from patrimonial land (becoming "landless") or legally redefined as a tenant." See also Neusner, *Politics*, 14–17, Fiensy, *Social History*, 5–6, Applebaum, "Economic Life," 662, Crossan, *Historical Jesus*, 223, M. Goodman, "First Jewish Revolt," 420–23, and Oakman, *Economic Questions*, 72–80.

8. Fiensy, *Social History*, vii.

9. Ibid., chapter 3.

10. Applebaum, "Economic Life," 631–700.

Because of the slender amount of hard evidence available, a debate persists in the literature about how much, in comparison with Judean peasants, the peasantry of Galilee was also stressed by these dual burdens of taxation and land expropriation. Goodman, for example, sees these economic stresses on the peasantry as much more intense in Judea than in Galilee. He writes, "[the] more distant areas of Palestine such as Galilee lacked such a wide division between economic classes."[11] Goodman goes on to criticize Freyne for unnecessarily adhering, in his 1980 book on Galilee, to the assertion of a struggle on economic and cultural lines in pre–66 CE Galilee between the urban centers and the inhabitants of the countryside. In his 1988 book, also on Galilee, Freyne asserts the need "carefully [to] differentiat[e] . . . Galilean conditions under Antipas from those in Judea under the early procurators," and goes on to describe how Galilee "was not at the time of the first revolt seething with disaffection and in a state of revolutionary turmoil," although "there were . . . *some* signs of disaffection in the region, manifesting themselves in acts of brigandage and thereby pointing to changes taking place within the economic balance."[12]

Edwards, in arguing for less conflicted urban-rural economic relations in Galilee on the basis of evidence for reciprocally beneficial trade, skirts the issue of taxation levels and does not address the question of land expropriation.[13] Freyne cites a list of heavy tax burdens on the peasantry under Herod Antipas and then remarks, "In the light of this catalog it is surprising that taxation does not surface in our sources as a major issue in Galilee . . . [as it does in Judea]."[14] Freyne then comments on the vicissitudes of land ownership.

> In debate is whether or not there was an appreciable move [in Galilee] from small family-run holdings in which reciprocity was still the basic mode of exchange, towards a situation of land use as a revenue-generating resource . . . [L]and ownership patterns in Galilee were mixed—large estates . . . and small, family run holdings. Undoubtedly . . . pressure had come on these latter since the hellenistic age, as increased taxation and narrow margins in terms of yields left the small landowner increasingly vulnerable. Once a person was caught in the situation of having to borrow money for whatever reason, thus mortgaging their holding, it was

---

11. M. Goodman, "First Jewish Revolt," 417–18.

12. Freyne, *Galilee, Jesus, and the Gospels*, 156, 161–62, 166 (italics original).

13. Edwards, "Socio-Economic," 53–73. See, by contrast, Horsley, *Archaeology,* 73–76.

14. Freyne, "Economics of Galilee," 87–88.

> extremely difficult for them to recover . . . [W]hatever the ideal,
> the reality was that pressures on peasant ownership had increased
> considerably.[15]

In sum, for Freyne, "the market economy [in Galilee], far from bringing about an improved situation, was highly exploitative and created an obvious rift between the ruling elite and the vast majority of the population."[16]

Horsley gives an unusually precise summary of the tax burden on the Galilean peasantry of Jesus's time. He estimates that "Galilean villagers were subject to payment of imperial tribute, amounting to 12.5 percent a year under the Romans." In addition, "the Hasmonean high-priestly regime [in Jerusalem] almost certain[ly] subjected the Galileans to taxation . . . estimated as constituting over 20 percent of the crops." "The heavy Herodian taxation came on top of these two claims to the Galileans' produce . . . and continued under Antipas, whose revenue from Galilee and Perea was 200 talents a year."[17] Horsley observes:

> Powerful people . . . were in a position to gain control over land . . . primarily through the debt mechanism. State officials . . . priestly officers of the temple-state . . . commanding officers of garrisons . . . even middle-level officers in charge of a district or wealthy priestly families could gradually acquire control over lands and/ or their produce by virtue of their access to resources by making loans to desperate peasants. Certainly already wealthy and powerful figures could expand the land and labor they controlled by this means.[18]

One conclusion evoked by studying this debate is that Jesus was not observing a level of injustice so blatant as to provoke both rebellion and consequent Roman retaliation. Rather he was living within the rationalized "normalcy" of commonplace, everyday exploitation. Given the impact in the early first century both of decidedly high levels of peasant taxation and of a growing commercialization of the land throughout the empire (commercializaiton that increasingly moved peasant land ownership from an inalienable right to a transferable commodity), it does not require the presence of revolution or even social banditry to infer that in the Galilee of the

15. Ibid., 107–8.
16. Ibid., 118.
17. Horsley. *Galilee*, 217–18.
18. Ibid., 215.

20s and 30s there existed an ostensibly peaceful but nonetheless inexorably intensifying aristocratic expropriation of peasant land.[19]

Our Perceptions of the Master

Across the history of this parable's interpretation, the third slave's description of the master's very way of being, embraced and repeated by the master himself, has most often not been heard for what it is. Western listeners, steeped in the mores of modern capitalism, regularly miss how this man's mode of operating would have been perceived by the peasants in Jesus's original audiences as criminal. This aristocrat first chokes off any peasant protest, then raises his lone, powerful voice to impose his own, self-assured entitlement, and then, through his seemingly authoritative denigration of the whistle-blower, proceeds to mislead listeners down through the ages.[20]

How have we become so unable to recognize the precision with which Jesus here represents the endless process of elites and their co-opted retainers accumulating wealth at the expense of the vast majority from whom they take? How do we so readily locate ourselves on the side of those who steal?

. . . . .

Here we must pause and step back. If we look carefully at how Jesus has constructed his parable, we can discover with amazement that he has biased his narrative in favor of our *not recognizing*. With breathtaking artistry, Jesus imitates elitist control. His parable functions in exactly the same way as did the aristocracy of his day. It elevates the voice of the oppressor. It obliterates

---

19. See also Oakman, *Economic Questions,* 46–55; Crossan, *Historical Jesus,* 218–24; Fiensy, *Social History,* 77–79; Freyne, "Economics of Galilee,"107–8; Horsley, *Galilee,* 216–21; and Horsley, *Archaeology,* 76–85.

20. One possible criterion indicating which of the longer parables may be attributable to the historical Jesus is the presence of a *sustained* tension between its two major participants. Although of unequal status, within the confines of the parable these two are discovered to be evenly balanced in their frustrated efforts to have an effect upon the other. However, immediately following the parable of the Talents, the editor of Matthew, with the clear purpose of elevating the harsh master into a figure for God, disrupts this tension by having the last slave thrown "into the outer darkness" (Matt 25:30). What between the two protagonists had been a complex struggle for recognition, Matthew pulls apart into the more simplistic and less interactive categories of good and bad. (See also the Appendix.)

the voice of the oppressed. It supports the aristocrat's definitions. It allows into awareness no other perspective. It admires the master's final crushing of dissent. What better evidence could be had for the effectiveness of the parable's mimicry of imperial control? How better to envelop us in the irony of our own identification with the very persons who oppress us?

The Slaves

In this reading Jesus is using the metaphor "slave" to represent both the Jewish aristocracy and the Jewish retainer class, the latter consisting of bureaucrats, scribes, soldiers, tax collectors, and other prospering clients of the elite.[21]

Why, one has to ask, would Jesus, a devout Jew living in Israel, choose to characterize some of his fellow Jews as slaves? As metaphor, "slave" implies the gradual overwhelming of all resistance and the resulting incorporation of the conqueror's ideology. Those so controlled eventually surrender to mere compliance; imaginative opposition ceases. "Slave" has overtones of the well nigh irresistible penetration of one person's identity into the life workings of another. Now this is not a metaphor applicable in Roman-occupied Palestine to either Jewish Pharisee or Jewish peasant. Neither, whatever the force of the outsider's power, was ever tempted to incorporate that alien's ideology.

However, one group was, namely, the aristocracy and their co-opted retainers. Lured by financial and social rewards, this group had relinquished the egalitarian understandings of land distribution and debt alleviation inherent in the values of ancient Israel. "Slave," then, might well serve as metaphor for the insidious erosion of integrity threatening those Jewish elites thriving in the cities of Galilee through collaboration with Rome.

Supporting this hypothesis are the following observations:

—The Jewish revolt that followed the death of Herod the Great in 4 BCE led to the Roman destruction of Sepphoris, a city four miles distant from Jesus's native village of Nazareth, and to the selling of its inhabitants into slavery.

—Freyne writes: "There is no question that the population [of Sepphoris at the time of the first Jewish revolt (66–73 CE)] was Jewish, for Josephus sees its pacifism as a rejection of kinsmen.[22]

21. See chap. 2, n. 1.

22. Freyne, *Galilee from Alexander to Hadrian*, 123, citing Josephus, *Jewish War* 3:32.

—During Jesus's later childhood and early adolescence, Sepphoris was Herod Antipas's provincial capital. Its requirements for both sustenance and privilege, together with Antipas's program of rebuilding the city (to which was added between 17 and 20 CE the building of a new capital, Tiberias), placed a necessarily large tax burden on the surrounding peasantry. A major function of the Jewish retainer class in Sepphoris would have been to oversee the collection of those onerous taxes.

—Born around 6–4 BCE, and from a landless peasant family (and therefore on the margins of that village society), Jesus became a *tektōn*, a "skilled craftsman," i.e., a worker in wood and possibly also a builder and mason. Because the nearby city of Sepphoris was rebuilt by Herod Antipas during Jesus's later childhood and adolescence, Jesus almost certainly would have worked there.[23] He would consequently have had multiple opportunities to observe both the behaviors and the dilemmas of the Jewish retainer class.

The linchpin of empire is the collaboration of this retainer class; without them, governance in the Galilee could not function. This fact may seem obvious, but its implications are significant. Being essential, the retainers are also positioned to invoke change. Crossan observes that peasant resistance, lacking retainer leadership, cannot succeed.[24] Crossan also makes the point that the combination of dissident peasants and dissident retainer leadership, especially on the ideological level, is always dangerous.[25] Finally, Crossan argues for the existence of a "giant fault line" within elitist rule that extends into the retainer class, namely, the division between those who owed their loyalty primarily to the authority of the existing government and those who owed their loyalty primarily to the authority of divine mandate.[26] In creating his parable, where the first two of these retainers are unabashed collaborators but the third is not, Jesus is concentrating precisely on this fault line. In devising the character of the third slave, Jesus appears to be addressing those Jewish retainers in urban Galilee who might still

---

See also Crossan, *Historical Jesus*, 18; and Meyers, "Roman Sepphoris," 324–26.

23. See Kee, "Early Christianity," 15; and Duling, "Jesus Movement," 167, 169.

24. Crossan, *Birth of Christianity*, 166–68, following Kautsky, *Politics of Aristocratic Empires*, 304, 306.

25. Crossan, *Birth of Christianity*, 170.

26. Ibid., 171–73, following Lenski, *Power and Privilege*, 263.

possess some allegiance to the social egalitarianism so central to ancient Israel's values.

The Third Slave—and Parable Listeners

Between the master and the third slave stands no outsider, no third term capable of redefining and mediating the master's controlling definitions. (That work falls to the listener.) Under the avalanche of the master's overpowering assertions, the parable buries awareness of the third slave's carefully calculated challenge to his master's greed. Then, as if to magnify even further the master's assumed right to trumpet his self-serving definitions unimpeded, Jesus suppresses any evidence of this aristocrat's vast array of victims. He firmly excises any reference to the essential work of peasant farmers, day laborers, artisans, and slaves, who, taken together, are the empire's fundamental producers. He completely hides the painful, humiliating, and enraging experience of that great number of nameless others whom these powerful investor slaves must dispossess in order to make the obscene profits they proudly present to their lord. While praise flows lavishly to these subordinate exploiters, Jesus altogether silences the suffering, as well as the outrage, of those from whom they steal.

Why would Jesus so completely imitate the behavior of the oppressors? A partial answer might be that he thereby immerses his hearers inside an overpowering corruption similar to that endured by the third slave. Just as this aware subordinate must discover, squeezed within the massive pressures imposed on him by the aristocracy, the exceedingly limited options remaining, so listeners must find their way among similarly buffeting and constricting forces. A probable original target of the narrative, the ethically sensitive retainer, would be drawn toward puzzled appreciation, but never confronted.

The third slave, along with those listeners who are willing to follow him, appears to move either uncertainly or else deftly within a disguised resistance that aptly reflects the imperial domination of definition. His constricted, perhaps deliberately inarticulate, perhaps skillfully hidden, seemingly cowardly, apparently mocking, and always dangerous resistance becomes a necessarily misleading but nonetheless precise—and courageous—counterpoint to the dominating strategies so fundamental to the functioning of empire. Each of this subordinate's confusing moves in turn reflects empire's varied threats to the integrity of imagination and to the wholeness of body—threats that can so readily distort, disorganize, or even destroy independent thought and action. By choosing to locate themselves either against or with the third slave, parable listeners themselves adopt or resist these same distorting strategies so essential to imperial control.

LABORERS AND A VINEYARD OWNER

(The Vineyard Workers)

THE SITUATION

A landowner went out early in the morning to hire laborers for his vineyard.

SCENE I

After agreeing with the laborers for the usual daily wage, he sent them into his vineyard. When he went out about nine o'clock, he saw others standing idle in the marketplace; and he said to them, "You also go into the vineyard, and I will pay you whatever is right." So they went. When he went out again about noon and about three o'clock, he did the same. And about five o'clock he went out and found others standing around; and he said to them, "Why are you standing here idle all day?" They said to him, "Because no one has hired us." He said to them, "You also go into the vineyard

SCENE II

When evening came, the owner of the vineyard said to his manager, "Call the laborers and give them their pay, beginning with the last and going to the first." When those hired about five o'clock came, each of them received the usual daily wage. Now when the first came, they thought they would receive more; but each of them also received the usual daily wage.

SCENE III

And when they received it, they grumbled against the landowner, saying, "These last worked only one hour, and you have made them equal to us who have borne the burden of the day and the scorching heat." But he replied to one of them, "Friend, I am doing you no wrong; did you not agree with me for the usual daily wage? Take what belongs to you and go; I choose to give to this last the same as I give to you. Am I not allowed to do what I choose with what belongs to me? Or are you envious because I am generous?"

—Matt 20:1–15 (NRSV)

4

Laborers and a Vineyard Owner,
Iraqi Oil and the United States[1]

Why would a vineyard owner suddenly become generous to a group of day laborers he otherwise consistently deprives?

JUXTAPOSING JESUS'S PARABLE OF the Vineyard Workers (Matt 20:1–15) with United States policy on Iraqi oil risks offending twice over. It invites readers to entertain two unpalatable propositions side by side: first, that a seemingly generous vineyard owner, in relation to his laborers, is being anything but generous, and, second, that a seemingly generous United States, in relation to the Iraqi people, is being anything but generous. These two propositions, which both laborers and Iraqis may find self-evident, go against strongly held convictions. However, placing this parable next to a deeply disguised strategy, which for the first decade of the twenty-first century was so central to U.S. foreign policy, may contribute to appreciating how profoundly Jesus engages the complexities of the human condition.

Both this parable and the manner in which the George W. Bush administration pursued control of Iraqi oil can be seen to be about silencing, about how those in power disguise their domination, and about how those dominated are systematically deprived of their voice. *What* is going on can

1. This chapter was first published in the *Fourth R* 22.4 (July–August 2009) 3–6, 22. Used with permission. For many of its perspectives, and for the situation of the workers in particular, I am indebted to Herzog, *Subversive Speech*, chap. 5 and especially pages 84–90, where in turn Herzog relies on Schottroff, "Human Solidarity," 129–47.

be described simply: "You are stealing our labor." "You are stealing our oil." On the other hand, becoming able to *see* what is going on is much, much more difficult.

Our Difficulty Seeing The Stealing; The Parable

Listeners familiar with the context for this parable in Matthew's Gospel may have trouble trusting the full range of their feelings. The resentment of the early workers is founded on a widely accepted premise. Because we have worked longer, we should be paid more—and "more" is always relative; compared with whatever you pay *them*, you should be paying *us* more. Everyone, everywhere embraces this belief. However, because Christian listeners have learned to assume that the beneficiaries of the superior's generosity, the late-coming laborers, represent late-coming Christians who are the recipients of God's generosity, they tend to let go of their aroused sympathies for the longer-working early laborers.

Some listeners, however, find that their discomfort persists. Could it be that the early workers have other, more substantial reasons for their anger? Such listeners must maintain this suspicion in the face of the owner's conviction that he is a good person. He insists that the complainers have received everything they agreed to. Since he has been faithful to his promises, how can they question his generosity? Vigorously, he counters their objections by appealing to his goodness: "Are you envious because I am generous?" (Matt 20:15). The doubts of listeners wilt.

Our Difficulty Seeing the Stealing: Iraqi Oil

After Saudi Arabia, Iraq has the world's second-largest reserves of oil. There are 80 discovered oil fields, of which only 17, containing 40 billion barrels, are in production. Waiting for future development are 63 known fields containing 75 billion barrels. Iraq also has the world's largest unexplored potential. On top of its 115 billion barrels of proven reserves (10 percent of the world total), it is estimated to have between 100 and 200 billion barrels of as yet undiscovered oil. Not only are these reserves huge, they are mostly onshore, in favorable reservoir structures, and extractable at extremely low cost.

On November 15, 1999, Dick Cheney, then CEO of the oil services company Halliburton, told the Institute of Petroleum in London, "By 2010 we will need in the order of an additional fifty million barrels a day. So where is the oil going to come from? . . . While many regions of the world offer great oil opportunities, the Middle East with two thirds of the world's oil and the lowest cost, is still where the prize ultimately lies." Two years later, after President Bush appointed him head of an Energy Task Force to consider where long-term energy supplies for the U.S. would come from, Vice President Cheney reported, "By any estimation, Middle East oil producers will remain central to world oil security."[2]

Nonetheless, since 2001, former Vice President Cheney and former President Bush, along with the vast majority of political leaders in the United States as well as almost all of the media, have together maintained, with remarkable discipline, a nearly seamless refusal to acknowledge that the war in Iraq had anything to do with oil. According to the Bush administration, the idea that the invasion and occupation were a means for the U.S. to gain control over Iraqi oil is "nonsense" and "a myth."

Because he dared break this massive silence, an isolated statement by Alan Greenspan, former chairman of the Federal Reserve, instead of being obvious became newsworthy. "I am saddened that it is politically inconvenient to acknowledge what everyone knows: the Iraq war is largely about oil."[3] The White House met this assertion with ridicule; an administration official termed it "Georgetown cocktail party analysis." Such superficiality, according to this official, comes from the same high-level professional whose every public utterance across eighteen years functioned as the trusted underpinning of financial markets across the globe.

The Actual Stealing: The Parable

The vineyard owner's claim that he collaborated with his laborers in setting the usual daily wage ("Did you not agree with me for a denarius?") represents either self-deception or else deliberate insult. Given a market flooded with impoverished, unemployed laborers, the owner has to know that none of them can bargain with him. Indeed, no effort on their part to negotiate would have any effect on what the owner will pay; that amount turns out to be, of course, whatever the owner's social class long ago determined it

---

2. This and the previous paragraph are derived from Muttitt, "Crude Designs," 8–9. (See also chap. 1 n. 3.)

3. Greenspan. *Age of Turbulence*, 463.

would be. Following his momentary generosity, the owner will revert to paying the customary wage for a day's labor—that is, a denarius.

To understand what is going on, one needs to be informed about two realities, both well known to Jesus's early listeners: (1) In that era aristocrats systematically taxed, lent back the money, waited for default, and then foreclosed on peasant land, thereby forcing many small-plot farmers into the swelling class of expendable day laborers. (2) One denarius would supply enough food to sustain one agricultural worker for about ten days (estimating three thousand calories per day).[4] However, access to even this amount of food was immediately compromised by taxation, housing, dependents, other needs, and, crucially, the fact that agricultural day laborers could generally find work only at times of planting and harvest.

Jesus carefully portrays the inevitable consequences of these realities: at five o'clock in the afternoon the owner can still find unemployed day laborers in the marketplace (Matt 20:6). These men are so poor that they are willing, in their desperate need for work, to wait through the heat of the day and even into the late afternoon. Parables scholar William Herzog reminds us in the twenty-first century what every first-century laborer knew conclusively. "Because the day laborer worked so infrequently . . . a denarius a day would not [even] sustain life."[5] Taking advantage of a chronically high level of artificially imposed unemployment, the owner is legally stealing his workers' sustenance, the very foundation of their lives.

The Actual Stealing: Iraqi Oil

Drafted in July 2006, the United States' secretive policy on Iraqi oil is most clearly unmasked in the largely unpublicized *Iraq Oil Law*. A draft of this law was shown to the U.S. government and to multinational oil companies in July 2006. "The Iraqi parliament . . . would not see it until March 2007, eight months after its completion, when they were expected promptly to pass it into law."[6] Despite immense pressure from the U.S. across several years and four drafts, this proposed law has remained blocked in the Iraqi

4. Oakman, "Two Denarii," 36, 37.

5. Herzog. *Subversive Speech*, 90. Herzog further observes that Oakman, in "Two Denarii," "seems to assume 'the silver denarius of Roman vintage' rather than local variations of it" (ibid.). See also Fiensy, *Social History* 86–90: "We are probably forced to conclude . . . that the average day laborer lived in poverty and stood on the edge of hunger" (89).

6. Muttitt, *Fuel on the Fire*, 170.

parliament.[7] A majority opposes it and for good reason. If enacted, the law would give an unusually large proportion of the profits from at least three-quarters of the country's proven oil reserves to Western multinational oil companies.

The proposed law imposes three disastrous conditions on the Iraqi people:

1) It would give the Iraq National Oil Company exclusive control of only 17 of Iraq's 80 known oil fields, leaving the remainder of its known but as yet undeveloped reserves open to foreign exploitation.

2) The law would establish a Federal Oil and Gas Council with the power to review, change, negotiate, and approve the rights for exploration and production contracts. The law assigns membership on this council in a way that clearly violates Iraqi sovereignty. Side by side with the CEO of the Iraq National Oil Company are also seated executives of Western oil companies, empowered to participate on the very council charged with negotiating and approving contracts with their own corporations.

3) Most important, the law would legalize contracts known as Production Sharing Agreements (PSAs). While technically keeping ownership of oil reserves in state hands so that Iraqi sovereignty would appear intact, PSAs would in practice deliver to Western oil corporations rates of return that could range from 42 to 162 percent, far in excess of the usual industry return of 12 percent. For these reasons, Iraq's neighbors (Kuwait, Iran, and Saudi Arabia) refuse to make such PSAs legal. Generally subject to commercial confidentiality provisions and effectively immune from public scrutiny or legislative revision, these PSAs could lock the Iraqi government, now weak and under military

---

7. This chapter was written in 2008. For a more recent summary, prepared in July 2015, of the complex disposition of Iraqi oil, see "Iraq, Selected Issues." International Monetary Fund Country Report no. 15/236 (https://www.imf.org/external/pubs/ft/scr/2015/cr15236.pdf/.) Under part D, section 13 is the following statement: "The original hydrocarbon law, submitted to the parliament back in 2007, has not been approved due to disagreements among the various parliamentary factions." For an informed and engrossing account of the early history behind this long-standing and unexpectedly successful resistance, see Muttitt, *Fuel on the Fire*, especially 145–208. "A grassroots movement led by trade unions, oil experts, and subsequently political parties and religious groups succeeded in stopping the passage of the oil law, even when the world's sole superpower made it a top priority and sent additional troops [the "surge" of 2007] to assert its will in Iraq. This was an impressive and quite surprising achievement" (ibid., 329).

occupation, into highly unfavorable economic terms for up to forty years.[8]

Using carefully developed economic models, Gregg Muttitt of the human rights and environmental group Platform, which monitors the oil industry, has estimated that the imposition of PSAs (compared with keeping oil development in Iraqi government hands) would cost Iraq, over the lifetime of the proposed contracts, between $74 and $194 billion in lost revenue.[9] (Writing in 2005, Muttitt was using an oil price of $40 a barrel.) These figures may be compared with the estimated cost for the occupation, going into 2008, of $600 billion. The occupation is paid for by U.S. citizens; the oil profits would revert entirely to Western corporations. With this oil law the United States is trying to coerce the Iraqi government to acquiesce to Western control over the profits derived from two-thirds of Iraqi oil for at least four decades. Such a planned, secretive, ongoing effort at stealing has to rank among history's most egregious.

Being Deceived about the Stealing: The Parable

In this reading of the parable, Jesus is portraying the owner not as evil or cruel (any more than Americans are evil or cruel for consuming far more than their share of the earth's resources). Rather, he is imagining him as an aristocrat—that is, as someone with a learned entitlement. What is more important, by rendering him uncomfortable with his exploitation, Jesus also understands him as someone who still possesses vestiges of a Jewish heritage of justice seeking. If the owner were participating in his economic privilege without guilt, he would not go to all the trouble he does to craft a drama designed to reduce his unease. In an effort to compensate for his unjust ways, he will offer a fleeting charity.

8. *Draft Iraq Oil and Gas Law*, 15 February 2007 (https://en.wikipedia.org/wiki/iraq_oil_law_[2007]). For point 1 see Article 8, Section D. For point 2 see Article 5, Section C, subsections 5 and 6. For point 3 see Article 9, Section B, subsection 5. Because of the controversy surrounding PSAs, the term "Production Sharing Agreement" has been dropped in subsection 5 in favor of "Risk Exploration Contracts." RECs are the equivalent of PSAs under a different name.

9. Some of the assertions and language in this and the previous paragraph are drawn from Muttitt, "Crude Designs" 3–5, 16, 23. Concerning how much this law would cost the Iraqi people, Muttitt's is one of the more precise and extensive estimates to be found among the large array of articles posted on the Internet if one searches using the phrase "Iraq Oil Law."

Early on the owner conveys to some of his day laborers an ambiguous message: he intends to pay them "whatever is right." Translated here is the Greek word *dikaios*. Does he mean, in the word's Hellenistic sense, "what is right according to legal custom," or does he mean, in the word's Hebrew Bible sense, "what is just in the eyes of God"?[10]

The owner then spends considerable energy implementing his flawed drama. Instead of sending his manager to hire more laborers, he goes himself three more times to the marketplace. At the end of the day his efforts lead him to reverse the customary order in which laborers are paid. Herzog makes much of this reversal, rightly perceiving that in paying the last workers first, the owner is demeaning the worth of the earlier workers' only possession: their labor.[11] His need to humiliate some in the process of being generous to others can also be seen as evidence of anxiety about guilt in himself. A less conflicted, generous owner would have given everyone a proportionate bonus; a less conflicted, crass owner would simply have taken advantage of his workers' vulnerability.

However, this particular aristocrat cannot free himself from his ambivalent desire to fit into the Jewish norm of justice. Using a double negative, he returns a second time to his ambiguous claim to be just. To a protesting laborer he describes his actions with these words: "I am doing you no wrong." The verb here, *adikeō*, is from the same stem as the earlier *dikaios*. The owner's phrase literally means, "I am not doing to you what is not right," or, in the biblical sense, "I am doing you no injustice." Strip away the double negative and there remains an echo of his earlier seeming promise to be just.

·   ·   ·   ·   ·

Only near the parable's end does the owner finally abandon his earlier ambiguity. He says, "Am I not allowed to do what I choose with what belongs to me?" (Matt 20:15). Here he is no longer appearing to promise obedience to God's just ways; now he is declaring himself obligated merely to the far more malleable framework of what is customary and lawful. Almost imperceptibly, he has relinquished his seeming readiness to provide justice and

10. That the parable may play on the distinction between God's justice and the question of fairness within systemic injustice was first suggested to me by Kaylor, *Jesus the Prophet*, 133–34.

11. Herzog. *Subversive Speech*, 91.

instead has reverted to his commonplace aristocratic right to give—and to take.

The most convincing evidence for the owner's uncertainty about his own goodness comes at the very end; it is lodged in the degree to which he must resort to self-deception in his efforts to make himself appear honorable. Basing his claim on a momentary generosity subsidized by the completely inadequate wages he regularly pays, he has the arrogance to declare, face-to-face with the same laborers he is systematically impoverishing, that what they are feeling toward him cannot be rage; instead they must be feeling envy—because he is such a good person.

The owner is so preoccupied with bringing honor to himself that he remains oblivious to how much honor he has thereby stolen from his workers. Instead of having his laborers share equally in the benefits of their single possession, their labor, the owner engineers a drama in which for some to have more, others must have less—in this case, less dignity. For him to feel reassured that he is good, he has had to place into his unprotected workers, in addition to his usual depriving, a wholly gratuitous experience of shame.

Being Deceived about the Stealing: Iraqi Oil

The following two quotes are characteristic of former President George W. Bush's speeches concerning the war in Iraq:

> We're helping the people of Iraq establish a democracy in the heart of the Middle East. A free Iraq will fight terrorists instead of harboring them. A free Iraq will be an example for others of the power of liberty to change the societies and to displace despair with hope. By spreading the hope of liberty in the Middle East, we will help free societies take root—and when they do, freedom will yield the peace that we all desire. (March 19, 2008)[12]

> If people across the Middle East see freedom prevail in multiethnic, multi-sectarian Iraq, it will mark a decisive break from the long reign of tyranny in that region. And if the Middle East grows in freedom and prosperity, the appeal of extremism will decline, the prospects of peace will advance, and the American people will be safer here at home. (March 27, 2008)[13]

12. Bush, "Bush Remarks on Iraq War and Terrorism."
13. Bush, "Bush Asserts Progress in Iraq."

Former President Bush consistently told the American people that his war aims were to provide Iraqis with democracy, liberty, hope, freedom, prosperity, and peace. When facing critics in this country as well as in Iraq, he has the arrogance to say, along with the vineyard owner, "Are you envious because I am generous?"

The Consequences of Being Deceived about the Stealing: The Parable

Because the underlying inequalities on which he depends would not permit it, the owner's generosity cannot possibly produce substantive change. In a world of unequally distributed resources and less than subsistence daily wages, the owner cannot realize his possible ambition to "pay what is just" out of what "belongs" to him until much more of what belongs to his landowning class belongs to the day-laborer class. If one chooses to believe that in his desire to be good the owner aspires to justice, then at issue that evening is no longer a decision about the worth of a day's labor but rather a judgment about decades of land grabbing. For the owner truly to succeed in being generous, the entire social structure to which he belongs would have to be transformed.[14]

The owner is offering charity as if it were justice; the laborers are receiving deprivation as if it were generosity. By disguising his control, the owner's distorting gifts make difficult any coherent rejoinder. The laborers know something is wrong, but they do not have the words to say what it is. The real difficulty, the absence of divinely ordained justice, is a lack they cannot begin to imagine. Within the confines of the systematic deprivation they have always known, all they can complain about is that they are being treated unfairly—and even at that level they are stymied. How can they mount a convincing protest if the owner remains so generously in complete control?

Because his seeming magnanimity restricts his laborers' ability to resist, the owner can keep on believing that he has behaved honorably. His dominance ensures his ignorance; he exits convinced of his goodness. However, if in the long term those in power elevate themselves by humiliating those beneath them, such violence will eventually beget violence. Unchanged, the disguised violence in the parable of the Vineyard Workers will lead eventually to the open violence in the parable of the Wicked Tenants.

14. See Kaylor. *Jesus the Prophet*, 134–37.

The Consequences of Being Deceived about the Stealing: Iraqi Oil

Iraqi citizens by and large have little information about the massive theft the U.S. is attempting to perpetrate against them; nonetheless, they have long suspected it.

> In one of the first studies of Iraqi public opinion after the US-led invasion of March 2003, the polling firm Gallup asked Iraqis their thoughts on the Bush administration's motives for going to war. One percent of Iraqis said they believed the motive was to establish democracy. Slightly more—five percent—said to assist the Iraqi people. But far in the lead was the answer that got 43 percent—"to rob Iraq's oil."[15]

However, a small minority in Iraq is fully aware. The following is an excerpt from a statement by the Iraqi Federation of Oil Unions to the 2008 Chevron and ExxonMobil shareholder meetings.

> We demand that the U.S. government, oil companies and others immediately cease lobbying for the oil law which would fracture the country and hand control over our oil to multinational companies like ExxonMobil and Chevron. We demand that all oil companies be prevented from entering into any long-term agreement concerning oil while Iraq remains occupied . . . Only after all occupation forces are gone should a long term plan for the development of our oil resources be adopted.[16]

. . . . .

Failing to entertain the obvious, we resist even suspecting what these few Iraqi protesters know so well. Because we too want continued access to plentiful oil, we collude in the silencing orchestrated by our leaders. We accede to our government's definitions of what is happening. We agree that the prime purpose of our arms in Iraq was to establish democracy. We remain unwilling to recognize our government's collaboration with Big Oil to wrest control for themselves over vast amounts of Iraqi wealth. We go on believing that we are good—and if the Iraqi people oppose us, they must be

15. A. Goodman, "New Iraq Oil Law."

16. This statement was delivered by Hassan Juma'a Awad, President, Iraqi Federation of Oil Unions on May 30, 2008. (See Awad and Iraqi Federation of Oil Unions, "Letter to the Shareholders of ExxonMobil and Chevron Corporations.")

in the wrong. Along with the vineyard owner, we too have the arrogance to say, "Are you envious because we are generous?"

How Do We Listen?

Immersion in Jesus's parables can lead to a growing awareness that they enclose unintegrated ways of seeing. The point of view of the owner is altogether different from that of the workers. Lacking reciprocal speech, each parable protagonist has no way to grasp how the other sees things. Only the listener is positioned to perceive the very different perspectives of both sides. But often listeners grasp only one side—that of the superior. This shortcoming is occasioned in part because onto this blocking of reciprocal speech Jesus superimposes the appearance of accurate speech. The parable's final scene depicts the vineyard owner as the authoritative judge of what has happened. Because we in the West tend to listen from the point of view of privilege, we must struggle doubly hard to see the irony in how we have allowed ourselves to be misled by the very person we believe should be most able to lead us.

The fundamental reference point for Jesus's parables is found in his understanding of the kingdom of God—that is, the desire of God or the intention of God for the world—which in turn alludes to the way things would be if the world were ruled by God. Thus we are offered the question, Do we get peace through coercion and grabbing, no matter how well disguised, or do we get peace through equality and sharing? The kingdom of God says the latter. Never has this proposition been more urgently pertinent than in today's shrinking world. It may be that one way the kingdom of God begins to come, one way equal sharing for all begins to come, is to be found in how we listen to a parable.

A WOMAN WITH LEAVEN

Jesus [said],

(a) The Father's imperial rule is like [a] woman

(b) who took a little leaven, [hid] it in dough,

(c) and made it into large loaves of bread.

A WOMAN WITH A JAR

Jesus said,

(a) The Father's imperial rule is like a woman
   who was carrying a [jar] full of meal.

(b) While she was walking along [a] distant road,
   the handle of the jar broke, and the meal spilled
   behind her [along] the road. She didn't know it;
   she hadn't noticed a problem.

(c) When she reached her house, she put the jar down
   and discovered it was empty.

A MAN WITH A SWORD

Jesus said,

(a) The Father's imperial rule is like a person
   who wanted to kill someone powerful.

(b) While still at home he drew his sword and thrust it
   into the wall to find out whether his hand would go in.

(c) Then he killed the powerful one.

   —Thomas 96–98 (Scholars' Version)

5

A Woman with Leaven, a Woman with a Jar, and a Man with a Sword: Gender Inequities[1]

These parables, placed side by side, appear to draw together and balance three seemingly incompatible domains: creative collaboration within the limits of nature; catastrophic disaster which, because it is tinged with the barest hint of human responsibility, invites both blame and despair; and courageous, transforming coercion, the success of which renders an entire process vulnerable.

IN THE GOSPEL OF Thomas, three of the very shortest parables attributed to Jesus,[2] ones that might be titled A Woman with Leaven, A Woman with a Jar, and A Man with a Sword, are linked together as a group. The present chapter explores what might happen if this linkage is made a strategy for interpretation. Perhaps whoever early in the tradition yoked these three together understood something from which we might learn.[3]

Taking hold of this possibility, we may approach each narrative as if it were part of a triptych—that is, as if each were like one of the three panels

1. This chapter was first published in *Interpretation: A Journal of Bible and Theology*, Vol. 56, No. 3, July, 2002, 295–306. Used with permission.

2. Although few doubt the authenticity of the Leaven, there is debate about whether the two newly discovered Thomas parables were authored by Jesus. I offer, for the reader's evaluation, the hypothesis that the intimate manner in which each regularly plays off the other two constitutes persuasive evidence that all three are the work of the historical Jesus.

3. See the discussion of linkage in the Gospel of Thomas in Crossan, *Birth of Christianity*, 242–44. Crossan notes that "topical [concerning internal content] or formal [e.g., parables] complexes are very unusual in the *Gospel of Thomas* . . . catchword associations are much more usual" (243).

in those storytelling paintings often placed over the altars of medieval churches.[4] Based on the assumption that all three are created by the same masterful imagination, this strategy allows each to enter into dialogue with the other two, each to expand what in the other two might be muted, and each to balance what in the other two might be emphasized. One of these parables, A Woman with Leaven—appearing in Thomas 96; Matt 13:33; and Luke 13:20–21[5]—is familiar; the other two, found only in Thomas, are not.

Resonances

The first of these parables, the Leaven, is joyful and full of growth; the other two, for very different reasons, are painful and dark. If at some point they were taken together to represent some aspect of the kingdom or rule or desire of God, it is easy see why the painful two were dropped. Nonetheless, these three brief narratives appear related in ways that range from direct comparison to direct contrast.

All three narratives involve the inserting of something into a container; all three raise questions about how securely that container holds. In the Leaven what is inserted is familiar and benign; it causes a gradual change, resulting in a productive outcome. In the Jar what is inserted is an unidentifiable force, something altogether unknown; it causes the jar to break and its valued contents to be lost. In the Sword, what is inserted is well known and horrifying; it causes the spewing forth of death. Contrasts in content are complemented by contrasts in mood: quiet satisfaction stands next to bewildered humiliation, which in turn is contrasted with a combination of utter terror and aggrandizing pride.

What Happens to the Human Body

When one puts leaven or yeast into dough, the dough rises. This connotation is readily associated with pregnancy; the woman takes semen into her body, and her body mysteriously swells. With little capacity to control what

---

4. This suggestion is from Scott, *Hear Then the Parable*, 306.

5. Funk et al. follow much of the scholarly consensus when they write, "The Matthean and Lukan versions of the parable [are] . . . considered more original than the version in Thomas because the contrast of 'little leaven—large loaves' has been introduced into the parable by Thomas" (*Parables*, 29).

happens, she nonetheless becomes deeply gratified and gratifying. What is hidden matures slowly—and the outcome is a soft success.

In this regard the Jar may be seen as the Leaven's opposite: a story of barrenness or miscarriage.

This woman also has little capacity to control what happens, and the woman's supposedly full jar becomes empty; her body inexplicably fails to hold its contents. What is hidden malfunctions slowly—and the outcome is a hard failure.

The possibility that the dough and the jar represent a person's body is made explicit in the Sword, where the fate of the powerful man's actual body becomes central. Broken open like the jar, that body is punctured and, like the meal in the jar, its contents spill out on the ground. It can no longer function as a container; another body must take its place.

What Happens around Us

Contrasted with both the Jar and the Sword, the Leaven provides an example of human collaboration with nature that progresses easily towards completion. Here is neither the threat of disaster nor the uncertainty of overthrow; the future is in small doubt. All that is required of the participant is a modest, undemanding contribution; God will do the rest. The woman approaches her task with an experience born of generations. Not understanding how it works and not caring much about it, she confidently expects her result; those around her take her success for granted. The parable becomes a metaphor for the pleasures of human control within the limits of the natural order.

In the Jar a woman also approaches her task with unthinking confidence; paying little attention, she proceeds to do what she has always done. Suddenly, however, she discovers that what she had been assuming was intact and full has become broken and empty. Dismayed, she is left only with disappointment and anticipated humiliation, for others will soon blame her for her loss. In contrast to both the Leaven's quiet pleasure and the Sword's daring initiative, the Jar depicts the shock of catastrophe; enclosed within its boundaries is the experience of every person ever subjected to the inexplicable helplessness of unexpected insult.

In the Sword, an intensely calculating man, knowing full well his danger, tests and retests his steadiness of purpose. Then, screwing up his courage, he risks his life. To his great relief, he succeeds. At first others will either praise him or become enraged; then they will with caution watch him. His spoiling of the powerful man's body bespeaks the human tendency to destroy what contains us. The powerful man has embodied a communal cohesion now broken apart—destroyed in order to be reconstituted.[6] Any evolution of natural processes, whether slowly beneficent or unexpectedly catastrophic, is here overtaken by an assertion of human will; through his risk-talking initiative the upstart first tears down what he hopes later to refashion, namely, the very fabric of society.

What Happens to the Order of Things

In the Leaven, no worlds are at stake because none is challenged; it is unthinkable that the yeast will not act. Successful human initiative occurs within established certainties. Ranging from the expansion of the universe to the mitosis of a cell, these ongoing processes are simply assumed.

At first glance the Jar and the Sword appear joined at the hip, as it were, by the shared image of a broken container, of a body emptied of its life-sustaining contents. At the same time they look like precise opposites: the woman's passive helplessness contrasts vigorously with the man's courageous determination. Closer examination, however, reveals a more complexly textured contrast: the woman, who has done nothing wrong, is left immersed in shame while the man, a murderer, walks away erect with pride. (When these two parables are placed side by side, with what provocativeness do they reflect the gender inequities of the ancient, and modern, world![7]) From the perspective of a casual observer, the fate of the woman's jar appears trivial, whereas the fate of the upstart's thrust seems of great concern. From the perspective of either participant, of course, the outcomes of their differing ventures are of equal import; whether the result is miscarriage or disembowelment, worlds are at stake.

These three narratives vary widely in how they represent a sense of control. Contrasted with the more sharply defined success or failure of a woman's ability to contain, to bring to fruition, and to give birth is the far more ambiguous effectiveness of male courage to puncture, to destroy—and, by implication, to rebuild. For the new strong man, newly positioned, has yet to proceed; the shape of his particular intentions, promising or corrupt, remains obscure. Not known is whether he will maintain his present

---

6. A ready analogue in today's world is the destruction of Saddam Hussein.

7. For an overview of gender inequity in first-century Palestine, see Hanson and Oakman, *Palestine*, 24–26.

lawlessness or will submit to the rule of law. He may as readily destroy as create.

How Others Respond

In the Leaven, the woman's part is circumscribed; the desired reaction occurs outside her participation. No onlooker holds her responsible for anything beyond her initial collaboration; the rest is the work of God. Here, as earlier proposed, is a compelling metaphor for a successful pregnancy and also for the smooth, unexamined fulfillment of larger societal expectations. Others are grateful for the outcome, but few invest much effort in appreciating either the complex functioning of the leaven or the amazing intricacies of intrauterine development; most are content to take God's pleasing work for granted.

The second woman is as unable as the first to control what happens. Clearly neither potter nor woman intended the jar's handle to break. Just as the cause of the leaven's action is hidden within some unknown chemical reaction, similarly obscured is the cause of this catastrophe. Nonetheless, the question of who will hold whom responsible stays very much alive; unlike the source of success, the source of failure requires precise identification. Having performed this routine task so many times, ought the woman to have become aware of the leak? Ought she have been able, by paying closer attention, to perceive the nearly imperceptible lessening of her burden? Or was her mistake simply to have grabbed the wrong handle?

The parable's ambiguity on this point effectively portrays the way uncertainties about a victim's participation during trauma wedges open space for society's cruel judgments. Here is found a metaphor not only for a woman's inability to bear a child but also for society's inability to produce a fair judgment. In the male-dominated culture of that era, as well as in most others, men were the ones who controlled that judgment. *They* decide that any failed pregnancy must be the fault of the woman, *they* blame her for her broken jar, and *they* require her to respond with shame. These stronger men, to ease their own anxieties, create and then impose upon the broken woman a humiliation that, loaded on top of the trauma of her failed initiative, becomes a backbreaker; under its weight someone who might otherwise have survived collapses into unrelieved depression.

To move from these two parables to the third is to move from the world of women alone, through the world of women and men together, to the world of men alone. The parable of the Sword portrays a courageous, determined decision making that in most cultures is seen both as the province of men and as a major source of what is to be admired. The Sword appears to applaud the man for wresting himself into control; at least it may be assumed that his action will lead to a beneficent outcome. But is it so? A hidden irony seems insistent: if you capture power by the courageous use of force, are you not thereafter vulnerable to overthrow by that same courageous use of force? Where in this sequence lies your authority? Or have you, at great risk, merely reproduced through lawlessness the same lawlessness you thought you had overcome? What appears to be a seeming resolution may instead become the harbinger of endless instability. For those experiencing the benefits of the sword, the manner of its success and the future it portends can be unsettling indeed.

These three narratives, taken together, seem to be exploring dimensions both of control and limit. In the Leaven, limit is not an issue because the question is not raised; initiative occurs within the boundaries of the natural order. In the Jar, where loss is depicted as a function of what one almost certainly cannot control, the pull is in the direction of downplaying the reality of limits and instead resorting to a putting out and a taking in of inappropriate blame. In the Sword, by contrast, the pull is in the opposite direction—from feeling gifted (with success) to feeling entitled (to dominate). Despair resulting from the imposition of too burdensome a limit here yields, following the overcoming and then the overthrowing of limits, to the potential for an out-of-control pride.

A Woman with Leaven and Sarah's Progeny (Gen 18:1–19)

Because Jesus was so clearly immersed in his own Jewish culture, it seems an obvious strategy for interpretation to inquire into resonances between his stories and narratives in the Hebrew Bible. I offer three, beginning with the story of the divine messengers announcing to Abraham the conception and birth of Isaac. Here the "three measures of wheat flour" of Luke 13:21 and Matt 13:33 readily compare with the "three measures of choice flour" of Gen 18:6.[8]

---

8. "Three measures of wheat flour" translates the Greek of both Matt 13:33 and Luke 13:21, *aleurou sata tria*. According to the *HarperCollins Study Bible*, 1882, "three measures would contain about 50 pounds of flour, enough for over a hundred loaves of bread." The Greek New Testament lexicographers Arndt and Gingrich in their *Lexicon*,

One may begin, in the case of Abraham and his visitors, with the absence of leaven. While leaven may well be a pervasive symbol of impurity, it also implies unhurried time. Abraham's hurried preparation for his unexpected guests is, of course, paralleled by Israel's hurried (unleavened) preparation for the Passover. But, more immediately, Abraham's alacrity to extend hospitality ("Quick, three *seahs* of choice flour!"[9]) contrasts with God's slowness to fulfill his promise made earlier, in Gen 12:2, to make of Abram "a great nation." Sarah's barrenness now merges with God's inexplicable delay.

However, much more is at stake here than overcoming infertility. Whereas the descendants of Ishmael, Abraham's son by his slave Hagar, will become "a great nation" (Gen 17:20), the descendants of Isaac, Abraham's son by his wife Sarah, are purposed to become heirs of the covenant (Gen 17). In the narrative immediately following, the extraordinary meaning of Sarah's pregnancy is revealed. Yahweh is speaking: "Abraham is to become a great and populous nation and all the nations of the earth are to bless themselves by him. For I have singled him out, that he may instruct his children and his posterity to keep the way of the Lord by doing what is just and right" (Gen 18:18–19). Concerning the entrance into history of justice and righteousness, the long awaited offspring of Sarah are destined to become leaven to the world.[10]

A Woman with a Jar and A Nearly Empty Promise (1 Kgs 17:1–24)

This next narrative occurs at a time when God's covenant with Israel has reached its nadir—a far cry from the world-embracing effectiveness promised by God to Abraham. As the prophet Elijah is introduced, all that abounds is famine. The Phoenician god Ba'al has four hundred and fifty

---

752, citing Josephus, *Antiquities*, 9.85, equate the Greek *saton* with the Hebrew Bible's *seah*. The Hebrew Bible lexicographers Brown et al. in their *Lexicon*, 684, equate one *seah* with about 10.7 quarts; thus three *se'im* would equal about 32 quarts. By contrast Plaut, *Genesis*, 168, identifies the three *se'im* of Gen 18:6 as the equivalent of "probably about twenty-eight cups [or 7 quarts], an overgenerous amount for three guests. However, it may have been customary on such occasions to include the important members of the household . . . or to supply provisions for the way."

9. This and other translations from the Hebrew Bible are taken from Jewish Publication Society, *Tanakh: The Holy Scriptures*.

10. For some of the insights of this paragraph, I am indebted to Leibowitz, *Studies in Bereshīt*, 158–71.

prophets abroad in the land; loyal to Yahweh is merely a handful led by Elijah. An abandoned widow and her dying son become clear symbols of the covenant's faithful remnant that Elijah has been called upon to restore. They are discovered reaching, with nearly empty lives, into a nearly empty jar. Intervening at the last moment, Elijah speaks for Yahweh: "The jar of flour shall not give out and the jug of oil shall not fail until the day that the Lord sends rain upon the ground" (1 Kgs 17:14). Later, however, the widow's rescued son is discovered near death. Elijah, intervening a second time, cries out to Yahweh; "'O Lord my God, let this child's life return to his body!' The Lord heard Elijah's plea; the child's life returned to his body, and he revived" (1 Kgs 17:21–22). This narrative, in turn, becomes the curtain-raiser to the cliff-hanger that follows, where Israel's faithful remnant, at the last moment and with amazing success, is restored.

In a set of cognate narratives, the prophet Elisha is intermediary first in filling a woman's empty jars (2 Kgs 4:1–7) and then in filling a woman's barren womb (2 Kgs 4:16–17). But later the life of the woman's new son is in jeopardy; only through the prophet's appeal is the boy saved (2 Kgs 4:18–37).

These repeated themes, linking the near death of the beloved, long-desired heir with the courageous intervention of a prophet's solitary faithfulness (echoing the story of Abraham's near sacrifice of Isaac), brilliantly capture the precarious vicissitudes of Israel's engagement with covenant faithfulness and broken faith. Involving jars and wombs and children, this ancient linkage is adumbrated in the parable of a woman with a jar. However, comparing the story of Elijah with the parable of the Jar reveals starkly what is missing. Absent in the parable is any prophet able to intervene. Here brokenness has become, simply, brokenness.[11]

A Man with a Sword and Moses's Liberation (Exodus 3–15)

The sword is a story of the deep fear aroused in the face of overwhelming odds, of the effortful recovery of courage, of immense risk taking, and finally of success. It represents a distillation of the male hero's saga, from

11. See Scott, *Hear Then the Parable*, 308. "The parable of A Woman with a Jar reverses the 1 Kings story. Given the significance of Elijah in eschatological speculation and the prominent protection promised to widows, this parable's referencing of the Elijah story creates a real scandal. There is no prophet to come to the woman's aid, nor will her jar be filled. The kingdom is identified not with divine intervention but with divine emptiness."

Odysseus and King David to Mahatma Gandhi and Martin Luther King Jr. Of the many male heroes of the Hebrew Bible, Moses is at the forefront.

The exodus narrative, full of themes of oppression, resistance, bravery, and the final overthrow of the powerful man, is introduced by Moses's intensely ambivalent self-doubt. When confronted by Yahweh's command that he challenge the awesome power of Pharaoh, Moses boldly and repeatedly asserts his caution (Exod 3:11; 4:1, 10, 13; 5:22; 6:12, 30). Throughout the beginnings of his risk-filled odyssey, this leader is so fearful that he dares brave the anger of the Lord (4:13). He falters—so that his brother Aaron becomes the one who must hold out *his* arm (7:8–10, 19; 8:1–2, 12). However, by the time of the sixth plague (that of the boils), Moses begins to act on his own (9:10). At the denouement, when "the Lord hurls the Egyptians into the sea," it is Moses alone who "holds out his arm" (14:21, 27). As Israel is born into a nation, so born is the courage of its most illustrious leader.

A Woman with Leaven and the Parable of the Talents (Matthew 25:14–28; Luke 19:13–24)

Before synthesizing these parables' varied reverberations with the Hebrew Bible, taking a second tack, that of comparing the present parables with others by Jesus, also promises insight. Of the many directions available, I offer three, the first being a juxtaposition of a Woman with Leaven and the parable of the Talents.

Just as the woman buries her leaven in dough, so the last slave in the parable of the Talents buries his potential investment in the ground. But where she expects growth, he seeks merely safety. In the usual understanding of the parable of the Talents, the last slave is considered a coward. Because he seems to refuse risk, he becomes, in the eyes both of his master and of many listeners, an abject failure.

But what if at issue is not cowardliness but courage? To entertain this question requires listeners to reevaluate the true nature of his master's enterprise. Few contemporary Western observers grasp what was obvious to Jesus's original peasant audience: someone who was realizing profits of between one hundred and one thousand percent in the closed economy of Galilee (where more for one means less for others) would be seen as both greedy to the core and a criminal.[12]

12. See Rohrbaugh, "Peasant Reading," 35. See also Fortna, " Underclass Eyes," 214,

Whereas the woman entrusts her initiative to the limits of the natural order, this last slave is called upon to entrust his initiative to an economic order mired in corruption. It is not true, as his peers claim, that money *makes* more money. Money, unlike dough, requires human sweat to grow.[13] For this slave to gain in his master's regard, others must be diminished—so he will have none of it. He knows full well that hidden within the obscene profits presented by his fellows to their lord is the barely recognized, hugely exploited, and desperately deprived labor of endless numbers of unnamed peasants, artisans, and slaves.

The woman buries her leaven in a context free of compromise; she realizes a result uncontaminated by corruption. As she takes, mixes, and makes, she has the rare pleasure of being clean. This last slave, by contrast, is forced to take within corruption; bravely he refuses to mix and, with considerable success, makes nothing. Although there is no need, in approaching the Leaven, to displace the traditional interpretive emphasis on impurity, when one puts this woman's task of burying within the natural order side by side with the dilemmas of this slave who must bury within *his* world of corruption, new questions may be raised about where the impurities might lie: how much inside the processes of nature, and how much inside those of human imagining? Elsewhere Jesus proposes that the destitute are blessed. The reason, according to Crossan, is not because they are better than the rest of us, but because within the pervasive structures of systemic injustice, they are the only ones left who are innocent.[14]

A Woman with a Jar and the Parable of the Prodigal Son (Luke 15:25–32)[15]

Just as the woman with the jar does, so the younger son carries a leaking vessel; only this one is not *on* his head—it is *in* his head. As onlookers watch with feelings ranging from amusement to amazement, the money from the young man's inheritance slips imperceptibly through his hands. Appearing utterly profligate, he is in fact utterly unaware. When finally he puts down his jar he discovers, to his shocked dismay, that it is empty. And through the

---

218; Cardinal, *Gospel in Solentiname*, 4:39–40; Kähler, *Jesu Gleichnesse*, 171–73; and Herzog, *Subversive Speech*, 160–61.

13. This insight is compellingly presented in Ngũgĩ, *Devil on the Cross*, 85.

14. Carlson and Ludwig, eds., *Jesus and Faith*, 154.

15. Chapter 8 develops in depth the following interpretation of the Prodigal.

centuries almost every listener to his story, akin to almost everyone who surrounds the woman, loads this young man with shame; he is the one, singularly and clearly, who must be forgiven.

The matter of who is responsible for this tragedy, so difficult to penetrate in the Jar, may be equally opaque when approaching the parable of the Prodigal. It is simplest to scapegoat the boy. To suspect otherwise requires one to scrutinize the father, a man is so universally assumed to be a figure for God as to render his motives sacrosanct. Few choose to suppose that what is leaking may also be within this father. As the son tries to leave home, could it be that he is carrying a cracked covenant between his father and himself—one no longer capable of sustaining his growth?

To enter into this astonishing possibility one must return to the very beginning of the parable, to the father's initial response when confronting his son's imperious demand. Why does not this generous father support with a substantial gift his son's intent to emigrate, instead of impulsively giving up control of his *entire* economic future to *both* his sons? Few fathers in any culture, in any era, behave this way. What impact might this sudden unloading of paternal responsibility have upon the weakly developed identity of this younger son?

Where one decides to position the son may depend on where, in this parable, one chooses to locate God. If one lifts God from some sole locus within the father and allows oneself to become more uncertain about where God is, one can also become a little more bewildered about where to place the blame—and whom to forgive. One may instead decide to sit down for a while and try to join the woman with her empty jar.

A Man with a Sword and the Parable of the Tenants
(Mark 12:1–8; Matthew 21:33–39; Luke 20:9–15, and Thomas 65)

Because the tenants pick up the sword, they will, like other rebels caught within the vise of the Roman Empire's *pax*, certainly die by the sword. That much is clear. What is so very unclear, however, is how the tenants cannot see this inexorable disaster coming. They are blinded because their stupidity is mirrored, exactly and step for step, by the stupidity of the landlord. The tenants wound the landlord's slaves (that is, besmirch his honor), and he, instead of being enraged, insists with incomprehensible obtuseness that the tenants have simply failed to recognize his messengers as from himself. Finally, fully informed of his tenants' foolhardy but dangerous rebellion, this landlord nonetheless determines to send his son into their midst un-protected. How can *he* not see the inevitable result that will follow? Unless you interpret this parable allegorically, and thereby relieve its tension by making the landlord a figure for God, you are in trouble; naked of allegory, the behavior of *both* parties appears to make no sense.

No one in this story started out as a murderer. The landless workers want greater control over the produce of their labor; the landlord insists that his degree of control, long since declared legal, is fair. Because he has become so accustomed to cloaking his greed under the guise of law, the landlord actually believes his tenants will abide by law. Because they so need to be unaware of their own weakness, the tenants actually believe their landlord is weak. Neither set of participants, in their insistence on what they imagine, notices the facts on the ground, namely, who actually has the power. Here, within this blindness on both sides, the tragedy is nurtured. Because the tenants have been seduced by the landlord's inappropriate be-havior to believe in their illusory power, everything in this tragic narrative becomes short-circuited; the tenants bite the unintended bait, the trap falls, the father is bereaved, and the tenants are dead.

The parable requires of its listeners to put some effort into answering the following question: Who is responsible for all the murders? Put another way, what in fact undermines the tender chances for justice? Parsed out next to the parable of the Sword, the parable of the Tenants displays in de-tail the ambiguities packed into the former, namely, the uncertain configu-rations of just or unjust swords operating under just or unjust laws. When the courageous man kills the powerful man, is his potent thrust capable of justice? Or is it merely wanton? Where does its authority lie?

These Three Parables and the Kingdom of God:

The kingdom of God, or how God would rule the world, may be partly described as how God longs for humans to act. We have little difficulty perceiving God's desire for creation. We know full well, for example, that being able to eat is better than starving, that breathing fresh air is better than breathing polluted air, that caring for children is better than abusing them: in short, we readily respect all the varied dimensions of the Golden Rule. But we have huge difficulties bringing these perceptions into reality.

Especially, we may ask, what characterizes God's rule, God's desire, when natural fecundity yields to bewildering devastation or to aggrandizing assertion? I propose these three parables placed side by side explore both the trustworthy self-limiting of God's intervening and the need for trust implicit within the limits surrounding human choice. The Leaven portrays the functioning of trust within lawful limits. The Jar goes in the direction of the pressures on trust that accompany debilitating catastrophe. The Sword goes in the opposite direction—toward the breakdown in trust essential to the violent achievement of success.

These parables are developed within the Hebrew biblical tradition. There, in related stories, the fundamental actor is God. Sarah's magnificent fecundity, both physically and ethically, is purposed by God. God intervenes to rescue and restore his beleaguered remnant. God is present within the enormous danger as well as the enormous victory of the exodus. And yet God waits, chooses to wait, for human responsiveness: for the faithfulness of Abraham, for the risk taking of Elijah, and for the courage of Moses.

Having granted humans freedom to choose, God yearns for the creation, through human participation, to develop well. And sometimes it does; sometimes, as does the woman with the leaven, we humans make the appropriate provision, and the creation thrives. The Leaven may well describe how human initiative can intertwine with nature in acts of creativity available to anyone willing to contribute within the limits of the created order.

The Jar, by contrast, contains a brilliant ambiguity. Ought the woman to have noticed that her burden was becoming ever so imperceptibly lighter? Should she have been paying that close attention? Is she responsible? At the same moment the woman discovers her "failure," others use her brokenness to impose upon her a humiliation that enables their own escape. The Jar thus leads towards the double desolation of any and every person experiencing catastrophe—whether from disease, disability, natural disaster, or poverty. As the rest go forward, yeasty and excited, these others, twice dispossessed, are left to contemplate the empty options of bitterness and being blamed.

But here may reside an even deeper irony. What if God is the one watching the woman who carries the jar? Ought *he* to be doing more? Ought *she* to be intervening? For certainly God, the sum of all goodness, longs that his creation, under the hand of humans, not miscarry. What is the feeling of God as she watches us carry our jar, our Earth, while it slowly leaks away? Is it like the feeling of the listener who watches the woman with the jar proceed without knowing what she is losing? Thus the Jar may be seen as standing squarely between the Leaven and the Sword, and challenging both. Is it indeed possible for God to allow her reign to miscarry so that God stands back and lets us come up empty?

When we consider God's reliance on human initiative, we are tempted to rush to the side of assertiveness. A Man With a Sword slows us down. It subtly asks, how can justice be established through courageous violence without falling prey to corrupting coercion? Because we are limited in what we can understand, violent victory invariably introduces bias. This parable raises the ominous possibility that an ongoing creative process—one that might have become more balanced through difficult collaboration across difference—may instead be undermined by a victorious defeating that in turn puts in place an intolerable distortion. Put more strongly, if we destroy (rather than transform) the powerful other, we run the risk of rendering ourselves vulnerable both to further destroying and to being destroyed. (One great twentieth-century example of this sequence is how the vengeful victors of World War I ensured the horrors of World War II.) In short, how can the oppressed evade the awful possibility of *themselves* becoming oppressors?

How do we pick up the Leaven, the Jar, the Sword? How do we carry them? How do we put them down? We can take one further step and notice fearfully where it leads us, and where it leaves God. The history of nonviolent protest, built on the history of Jesus's crucifixion, suggests that within the Sword may lie further irony. What if the truly courageous man is not the one wielding the sword? What if he is the one receiving it? What if that powerful man knows full well what is coming? What if he anticipates deliberately absorbing it? What if it is also *he* who goes into *his* house and there imagines taking that sword into *his* body?

A SLAVE AND A MASTER

(The Unforgiving Slave)

THE SITUATION

A **master** . . . wished to settle accounts with his slaves.[1]

SCENE I

(a) When he began the reckoning, one who owed him ten thousand
    denarii was brought to him; and, as he could not pay, his lord
    ordered him to be sold, together with his wife and children and all his
    possessions, and payment to be made.
(b) So the slave fell on his knees before him, saying, "Have patience with
    me, and I will pay you everything."
(c) And out of pity for him, the lord of that slave released him and forgave
    him the debt.

SCENE II

(a) But that same slave, as he went out, came upon one of his fellow slaves
    who owed him one hundred denarii; and seizing him by the throat, he
    said, "Pay what you owe."
(b) Then his fellow slave fell down and pleaded with him, "Have patience
    with me, and I will pay you."
(c) But he refused; then he went and threw him into prison until he would
    pay the debt.

SCENE III

(a) When his fellow slaves saw what had happened, they were greatly
    distressed, and they went and reported to their lord all that had taken
    place.
(b) Then his lord summoned him and said to him, "You wicked slave! I
    forgave you all that debt because you pleaded with me. Should you not
    have had mercy on your fellow slave, as I had mercy on you?"
(c) And in anger his lord handed him over to be tortured until he would
    pay his entire debt.

—Matt 18:23–34 (NRSV)
(author's changes in boldface)

1. See footnote 1 of chapter 2.

6

A Slave and a Master,
Main Street and Wall Street[2]

Why would a slave competent enough to secure a huge loan be stupid enough to cashier a colleague within easy view of his recently compassionate lord?

JESUS'S PARABLE OF THE Unforgiving Slave (Matt 18:23–34) invites listeners to engage a hidden complication. The extraordinarily generous slave master becomes enraged when his slave does not imitate him. However, never for a moment does this lord suppose that his subordinate, when grabbing and choking his fellow, *is in fact imitating him*. Sidestepping this complication is sometimes seen as the price one must pay to have the parable fit a certain interpretation. What if, instead, we embrace this difficulty? What new understandings might emerge if we take seriously the possibility that the slave, when being so astonishingly mean-spirited, is doing exactly what his master, until this very moment, has always done? Given the suddenness of his master's shocking change, the slave has not yet been able to assimilate this new, strange, and unexpectedly releasing lord; instead his imagination remains governed by a lifetime of experience with his old, familiar, and chronically domineering master, the one who never once loosened his grip.

---

2. This chapter was first published in the *Fourth R* 24.3 (May–June, 2011) 15–20, 22. Used with permission.

A Beginning Caveat

Before entering the parable, one must stop and question the impossibly huge loan of ten thousand talents. If the amount stands as written, the narrative becomes fantastic. Herod Antipas, who was able to impose on Galilee and Perea an annual tribute of about two hundred talents, would have been fifty years repaying.[3] Such hyperbole, however, clearly supports Matthew's allegorical interpretation; he understands the parable to be describing both how a gracious God forgives and how Christians in response ought also to forgive. Martinus C. DeBoer proposes that in order to enhance his allegorical reading, Matthew has vastly inflated the amount owed by altering a single word. He has changed the original "denarii" into "talents," and then promoted the slave master into a king.[4] I have agreed with deBoer and, using boldface, have edited the text accordingly.

Default on the Loan: The Parable

> A **master** . . . wished to settle accounts with his slaves. When he began the reckoning, one who owed him ten thousand **denarii** was brought to him . . . He could not pay . . .

The parable opens with an abrupt revelation; a previously reliable slave cannot repay a large loan. (To earn ten thousand denarii a day laborer, working every day, would need over twenty-seven years.) The master suddenly becomes aware he has lost a major investment.

As in other of Jesus's parables (the Wicked Tenants, the Talents, the Dishonest Steward, and the Prodigal Son), a wealthy superior's extending the use of his resources to chosen subordinates indicates both trust and an expectation of competence. Here, as in these other narratives, such hopes are dashed. At this signal moment of disappointment, listeners are beckoned both backward and forward in the narrative. What might have happened in the past between superior and subordinate to contribute to the present remarkable breakdown? How will the superior now respond? How will his response suggest what might have gone wrong in the first place?

---

3. Josephus, *Jewish Antiquities* 17:318–20.

4. DeBoer, "Ten Thousand Talents?" 214–32.

Default on the Loan: Wall Street

The novel interpretive possibilities offered by this story may become more persuasive when placed alongside recent events in the U.S. financial industry.

This latter narrative begins in the several decades prior to 2008. Deep in the bowels of large Wall Street investment firms, extremely smart and highly motivated executives-to-be are devoting all their energies to crafting immensely complicated, difficult-to-understand, moneymaking, constantly changing, and seemingly enticing financial instruments that will later be designated as "toxic." Far from Wall Street, in a lower-middle-class section of Baltimore, a hardworking high school teacher, having purchased a deliberately deceptive subprime mortgage on initially attractive terms, finds himself and his young family inexorably squeezed. Because his mortgage rates have risen precipitously, he cannot meet his payments, and the bank repossesses his home. He is then forced to watch helplessly as boxes of his children's toys are carried out onto the street. Across a great gulf in empathy, Wall Street executives stand aloof, focused on the abstract numbers flitting across their computer screens, watching only for evidence of increases in their already substantial wealth. Decades of deregulation and of the unsupervised merging of traditional banking functions with Wall Street trading have eliminated almost all outside control over the rapid expansion of this high-level, legalized, and unfeeling greed.

However, by the middle of September 2008 these investment strategies had led to an expanding potential for institutional default so large as to threaten the collapse of the entire financial system. In the space of days, investors began to suspect that many of the largest Wall Street brokerage firms, in debt to them for vast amounts of money, might not be able to meet their obligations. Confidence was eroding rapidly; a worldwide panic was imminent. Investigative journalist Andrew Ross Sorkin summarizes the complex events leading up to this sudden, massive meltdown.

> In 2007, at the peak of the economic bubble, the [U.S.] financial services sector had become a wealth-creation machine, ballooning to more than 40 percent of total corporate profits in the United States . . . Those who worked in the finance industry earned an astounding $53 billion in total compensation in 2007 . . . But while they were busy producing these dizzying sums, the big brokerage firms had been bolstering their bets with enormous quantities of debt. Wall Street firms had debt to capital ratios of 32 to 1. When it

worked, this strategy worked spectacularly well . . . When it failed, however, the result was catastrophic . . . [By September of 2008,] in a period of less than eighteen months, Wall Street had gone from celebrating its most profitable age to finding itself on the brink of an epochal devastation. Trillions of dollars had vanished.[5]

Failure to Anticipate Default, Leading to Extreme and Conflicting Options: The Parable

As he could not pay, his lord ordered him to be sold, together with his wife and children and all his possessions, and payment to be made. So the slave fell on his knees before him, saying, "Have patience with me, and I will pay you everything." And out of pity for him, the lord of that slave released him and forgave him the debt.

Assuming the slave borrowed the money in order to make money, slave and master have much in common. Both are enmeshed in a culture of greed. Both are operating within a closed agrarian economy where increasing the wealth of a few necessarily means depleting the resources of the many. Both have discovered how to extinguish awareness of the pain they are causing. As a consequence, loyalty to those within the fraternity of greed comes into tension with the ruthlessness inherent in having learned to ignore the distress of one's victims. What happens if your colleague in greed falls outside the charmed circle of success? Do you move to eradicate him, or do you work to rescue him?

By not anticipating the default, the master has squandered any chance he might have had earlier in the day to avert it. For whatever reason, he has not paid attention to the disguised warnings of distress coming from his increasingly desperate subordinate. At this end stage he has already forfeited a wide array of options that would have allowed him to intervene in more disciplined as well as more supportive ways, ones at once less harsh as well as less rescuing. Forced by his prior inaction to confront a *fait accompli*, the master has at this point restricted himself to only two options: He can either cut his losses by selling the slave and his family,[6] or he can rescue his formerly trusted subordinate by releasing him from his debt. Each option

5. Sorkin, *Too Big to Fail*, 3, 4.

6. Jerimias, *Parables*, 211 estimates that "the average value of a slave was about 500 to 2,000 denarii."

contradicts the other. Both are from the top down. Both require nothing from the recipient except abject submission.

Failure to Anticipate Default, Leading to Extreme and Conflicting Options: Wall Street

It turns out that precisely these two extreme and opposing options were also the only ones available to the government at their own very late, eleventh hour. Partly because of three decades of deregulation, in turn supported by an ideology of not interfering with what many took on faith to be "free" markets; partly because successive administrations had already provided implicit bailout guarantees to the huge, quasi-governmental mortgage holding companies Fannie Mae and Freddie Mac; and partly because of the immense and seemingly endless success of the economic model in place, the government had neither anticipated the impending disaster nor, what is more important, developed the political will to take the difficult steps necessary to avert it.

At this end stage in the crisis two government officials in particular had the authority to make the major decisions: Henry Paulson Jr., secretary of the treasury, and Timothy Geithner, president of the Federal Reserve Board of New York. In the space of forty-eight hours, these two men exercised *both* of their only two remaining options, each extreme and each conflicting with the other. On September 15, 2008, they refused to lend the billions needed to rescue Lehman Brothers, forcing that venerable institution into bankruptcy. On September 16, however, they completely reversed course and offered to provide $80 billion of taxpayer money to bail out the seriously ailing American International Group (AIG).

This government flip-flopping was in response to two equally unpalatable options: 1) Allowing any large Wall Street brokerage firm to enter bankruptcy would result in widespread loss of investor confidence, with the potential to provoke a panic that would sink neighboring institutions and thereby threaten the entire financial system. 2) However, rescuing troubled firms created equally serious dangers. One was provoking voter rage and backlash. A second, less evident to the public, was how government intervention on behalf of one large firm would signal to all the others that from now on they would be protected from untoward consequences should they continue to take excessive risk.

How Generous Rescue Does not Result in Generosity: Wall Street

Within weeks, the $80 billion taxpayer bailout proposed by Paulson and Geithner ballooned into the $182 billion rescue package approved by Congress in October 2008.

With the bailout of AIG, the die was cast. Because of the implicit government guarantee now in place to rescue firms "too big to fail," the surviving large investment conglomerates were able to garner loans in the marketplace at rates considerably lower than those available to their smaller, unprotected rivals. Since nothing in the regulatory context had changed, these large firms, with access to added capital, could continue to take exactly the same excessive risks that led to the crisis in the first place. Heads, we reap enormous profits; tails, the taxpayer picks up the tab.

In the months that followed the $182 billion taxpayer rescue of the big banks, unemployment rose, home foreclosures grew, and businesses could not borrow. By contrast, between October 2008 and February 2009, six hundred of the nation's top bankers paid themselves $2.03 billion in bonuses, for an average of over $3 million each in additional compensation.[7]

Public outrage was intense. "We lent you over $180 billion. We rescued all of you, directly or indirectly, from disaster. And what did you do? Did you think of how much we did for you? Did you work to extend a hand of rescue to us just as we extended a hand of rescue to you? Not for a minute. You did nothing to create jobs. You did nothing to prevent foreclosures. You did nothing to free up credit. Instead, all you did over the past five months was to grab more than $2 billion for yourselves."

What is surprising here is not that these financial executives proceeded to do these things but that anyone was *surprised* that they proceeded to do these things. To such outrage, roiling across the country, any close observer of Wall Street would respond, "What's the matter with you people? What in the world did you imagine these multimillionaire barons would do except keep on taking more and more for themselves? Did you really think they would pause, even for a moment, from their all-consuming greed in order to consider *your* needs? Surely you didn't expect that your unprecedented, stupendous act of generosity would actually *change* them, did you!"

---

7. Dash, "Federal Report Faults Banks."

How Generous Rescue Does not Result in Generosity: The Parable

With this example in mind, we return to the parable. Slave and master, unlike financial industry executives, are not only enmeshed in a culture of greed, they are also trapped in a culture of slavery. (It is as if Jesus is using the coercive greed of the one to reinforce the coercive control of the other.) What might the consequences of this dual entrapment be for slave, for master, and for parable listener?

The Slave

> And out of pity for him, the lord of that slave released him and forgave him the debt. But that same slave, as he went out, came upon one of his fellow slaves who owed him one hundred denarii; and seizing him by the throat, he said, "Pay what you owe." Then his fellow slave fell down and pleaded with him, "Have patience with me, and I will pay you." But he refused; then he went and threw him into prison until he would pay the debt.

One way to reenter the narrative at this point is to notice the slave's dangerous disregard for his own safety. The listener then has the option of moving from being impressed by the slave's failure to imitate his master's generosity (the place where most understandings of this story focus) to pondering the slave's monumental stupidity. Although well placed and skillful enough to win from his master a huge loan, this competent man, concerning a simple matter, makes an awesome mistake. Having just been released from debt, destitution, and possible destruction, he cashiers his fellow slave in easy view of his recently magnanimous lord. Not only is he unable to connect what has just been done for him with what he should now be doing, but he fails to anticipate how his refusal to mimic his master will inevitably provoke his master's rage.

The slave's unusually thoughtless and dangerous behavior makes sense only if an imagined reality takes precedence over the one immediately apparent. This slave's seeming stupidity may in fact represent his complete confusion. Throughout their lives both men have served the requirements of a society of slaves and masters; until now neither has relaxed the control essential to its maintenance. Each knows well how to shut out fellow feeling in order to crush the weaker other. Such ruthlessness was commonplace up and down the entire social spectrum; no one would have thought to raise a finger in protest.

After a lifetime of immersion in such unchallenged ruthlessness, the slave is utterly unprepared for his lord's shocking magnanimity; he simply cannot comprehend it. If the world is no longer made up of "users" and "used," of what could it possibly be made? If this slave master will no longer maintain the established order—the order that until this moment has contained *all* of the possibilities for prediction—then this slave, ignoring his personal safety, will reach out and wrench that order back into place. Where the master believes he has released, the slave may in fact feel swept away. As this sudden, unexpected riptide starts to pull him out to sea, the slave tries to hang on to the only trustworthy way of relating he has ever known; he grabs for his colleague's throat. He must pull back into place those long-standing patterns of greed and control that have always been the bedrock of his reality. When he chokes, demands, and imprisons, the slave is in fact imitating his master. However, it is not this incomprehensible, "new" master he now reaches for, but rather the merciless lord he has always known.

The Slave Master

> His lord ordered him to be sold, together with his wife and children
> . . . Out of pity for him, the lord of that slave released him and forgave
> him the debt . . . In anger his lord handed him over to be tortured . . .

The rapidity of the slave master's shifts in mood is breathtaking. Within a brief span of time he moves from the cruelty of breaking up a family (brooking no delay) to compassionate release (providing extraordinary largess) to vengeful torturing (allowing no escape). How can such different attitudes arise in such rapid succession from within the same person? One answer, in brief, is that the master tried to take a shortcut to achieve change—and got slammed.

By forgiving the debt the master makes an extraordinary gesture, both in its novelty and its risk. His action challenges entrenched practice; among his slaveholding peers he puts his reputation on the line. But the master also appears enticed by the supposed potency of his initiative. His explosive anger at the failure of his generous act suggests how convinced he is of its effectiveness. What may account for his shifting moods may be an inaccurate expectation born of dominance. For he indeed seems to hope, with surprising naivete, that with a single, masterful stroke he should be able to dent and even flatten those misshapen attitudes long hardened into the very foundation of a society of masters and slaves. (Main Street embraces similar expectations of Wall Street!)

This lord's manner of acting, surely appropriate to the behavior of slave masters, is ill fitted to the work of releasing. By remaining the sole arbiter of the new order as well as the old, he excludes any experience other than his own. By dictating rather than participating, he permits only compliance. By his generosity, he distances himself further from the realities of his own dominance. He attempts to release his slave's debt without acknowledging his own, namely, his obligation to recognize the utter contradiction between his newly minted releasing and his chronically insistent control. The master—and many listeners with him—simply assigns this backbreaking work to his slave.

Once within his new role as the one who releases, the master looks to his action to transform in a moment the harshness of a slave culture centuries in the making. Within the new, moreover, he retains the old; he still remains master. When releasing, he stays in charge. He does not wonder or ask; he declares. Precisely because he acts as master—that is, unilaterally—he cannot adopt what may be the only way available to him to enable his slave to change, that is, first of all to be aware of and affirm his slave's experience. The top-down nature of his initiative ignores his slave's need gradually to come to terms with a strange, dangerous, new way of being. By hoping to evoke a releasing attitude while remaining in control, the master undermines his own potency. Indeed, the master's condemning words, "Should you not have had mercy . . . as I had mercy on you?" appear very close to the words he has just condemned, namely, "Pay what you owe!"

The Parable Listener

One does not have to suppose that the master released the debt in order to render his slave a more generous person; nonetheless, both master and many listeners agree that such a transformation ought to have occurred. However, such listeners, along with the master and Matthew, are caught in a trap. They are supporting the very act the master has condemned, namely, the punishing of another for a failed obligation. Only this time the debt owed is not one hundred denarii but rather that the slave, whether he is ready to or not, imitate his master's unexpected generosity. Together with the slave master, these listeners say to the slave, "I will ignore your capacities in favor of my own expectations. I will imprison you until you repay an obligation that I have without warning or preparation decided to enforce. I will do to you exactly what I am punishing you for having done."

The slave does to his fellow what the master has *always*, until the most recent moment, done to him. Masters have *always* dominated slaves; this beast has careened down through the centuries unopposed. So who is responsible to halt it? This little guy at the end of the line? Does it in fact fall to this last to do the prodigious work that everyone before him has failed even to imagine, much less confront? The irony here is profound. This master—and many listeners with him—is saying to this slave, "You should be able to overturn in a moment what I have been unable to face in a lifetime," namely, the deep-seated attitudes of coercion that invade *both* parties when one person remains in complete control of another. When the master releases his slave's debt, listeners are drawn into having to make a truly remarkable choice. For at this moment they must decide whether this lord's singular act of generosity indeed has the power to wrest apart ancient slavery's iron law of ruthlessness.

Epilogue

If the parable is approached in these terms, the problems it offers are formidable. How indeed does one bring together the open-ended process of releasing with the human propensity to dominate? How is it possible to move the master's magnificent effort across the large gulf between the world of control, with its fixed requirement of compliance, and the world of releasing, where coercion necessarily dissolves in favor of first experiencing and then acknowledging how the other person feels? But how can the master possibly recognize the constricting effects on both himself and his slave of his own total immersion in the unchallenged corruption of a society of masters and slaves? How far, then, might the master's affronted rage be from its true source?

If we release our grip on the controlling interpretation of this parable, we may discover ourselves drawn to consider further the difficulties of entering the kingdom of God, or embracing God's rule, or participating in God's desire for the world. We may suspect we are being invited to experience more closely and plumb more deeply the complex dimensions of

Jesus' aphorism, "How hard it will be for those who have wealth [that is, for those whose lives are controlled by the ability to control others] to enter the kingdom of God!" (Mark 10:23).

A MANAGER AND A RICH MAN

(The Dishonest Steward)

THE SITUATION

There was a rich man who had a manager,

SCENE I

and charges were brought to him that this man was squandering his property. So he summoned him and said to him, "What is this that I hear about you? Give me an accounting of your management, because you cannot be my manager any longer."

SCENE II

Then the manager said to himself, "What will I do, now that my master is taking the position away from me? I am not strong enough to dig, and I am ashamed to beg. I have decided what to do so that, when I am dismissed as manager, people may welcome me into their homes." So, summoning his master's debtors one by one, he asked the first, "How much do you owe my master?" He answered, "A hundred jugs of olive oil." He said to him, "Take your bill, sit down quickly, and make it fifty." Then he asked another, "And how much do you owe?" He replied, "A hundred containers of wheat." He said to him, "Take your bill and make it eighty."

SCENE III

And his master commended the dishonest manager because he had acted shrewdly.

—Luke 16:1b–8a (NRSV)

7

A Manager and a Rich Man,
Afghanistan and the United States[1]

Why would a prudent estate manager, wholly dependent on his employer's goodwill for his security and even his survival, squander that goodwill?

OF THE PARABLES ATTRIBUTED to Jesus, the Dishonest Steward is widely held to be among the most difficult to understand. The impact of this story is most often located in one of two places: listeners are to emulate the later decisiveness (not the dishonesty) of the manager, or one's expectations are overturned by his employer's surprising commendation. These interpretations emphasize the behavior of one participant in isolation from the other. This chapter attempts to go in the opposite direction, namely, into the relationship between the two protagonists. It will use the position of Hamid Karzai, former president of Afghanistan, in relation to his patron, the United States, to illumine the position of the estate manager in relation to that of his patron, the rich man.

Hamid Karzai and His World

For United States policymakers, the war in Afghanistan was always an unwanted child. The reason this conflict was neglected in favor of its big brother, the war in Iraq, is straightforward. Afghanistan held only al-Qaeda; Iraq, on the other hand, holds vast amounts of oil.

---

1. This chapter was first published in *The Fourth R* 25.3 (May–June, 2012) 3–8. Used with permission.

America's rapidly improvised military response in Afghanistan to al-Qaeda's attack of 9/11 involved no U.S. troops; they had already been committed to Iraq.[2] Instead, the initial (and inconclusive) American victory against the Taliban was achieved on the cheap, paid for by CIA dollars given to Afghan warlords in exchange for the use of their soldiers. In the fall of 2001, when CIA director George Tenet, having judged him to be the Afghan leader most able to oppose the Taliban, decided to throw American support behind Hamid Karzai (who would later become president), it was the warlords, with CIA collusion, who were in control of much of Afghanistan.[3]

The Parable Manager and His World

We do not know how the man in Jesus's parable was chosen to manage the rich man's estate. However, we can tell from his behavior, both before and after his calamitous loss of position, that he possessed considerable ability. We also know that his employer, keenly aware of how to maximize his wealth, entrusted him with large amounts of both responsibility and authority.

The rich man is likely the owner of a landed estate; he needed substantial renters, contracted at substantial rents (paid in produce at the time of harvest), to make substantial profits.[4] Functioning within a competitive environment, his estate manager was expected to negotiate the most advantageous contracts possible. Moving among powerful men, he was the go-between, with everyone agreeing, however reluctantly, that it was his responsibility to make sure the rich man came out on top. The manager was effective; his later skill in feathering his own nest is clear evidence of his earlier skill in feathering his employer's.

The heightened suspicion endemic to almost every other relationship available to either man would render particularly gratifying the trust essential to their collaboration. These two envied and isolated coconspirators were in some ways tied together as a father and his son—or as a godfather and his lieutenant. Each required the other in order to function. Since for the manager such intense dependency occurred in a context almost totally

2. See chapter 1 n3.

3. See Rashid. *Descent into Chaos*, 74, 80–83, 127–36, especially 133.

4. For a detailed exploration of the various ways the manager's position and responsibilities might be understood, see Bailey, *Poet and Peasant*, 87–94.

devoid of other resources for security, he had to be highly sensitive to any hint of change towards himself in his patron's attitude.

Sowing the Seeds of Failure: Karzai

The British failed to conquer Afghanistan. So did the Soviets. In their turn, by deciding to intervene militarily in pursuit of al-Qaeda, the Americans became enmeshed in a conundrum so complex that it was probably beyond the ability of any invading power to resolve—namely, how to disentangle defeat of al-Qaeda (an Arab-led, foreign organization that had only recently secured a foothold in Afghanistan) from defeat of its indigenous ally and protector, the Taliban (a nationalist Afghan movement dedicated to achieving a modicum of social justice within a conservative and deeply corrupt society by imposing, however repressively and even cruelly, Islamic—or shari'a—law).

It is one thing to have as your goal the destruction of al-Qaeda; it is quite another to try to go head-to-head with the Afghan-based Taliban in an effort to win the hearts and minds of masses of impoverished Afghans. Having equated defeat of al-Qaeda with subjugation of the Taliban, the Americans never took full measure of the huge dimensions of the task they had undertaken. Not only must they overcome the stubborn nationalist opposition aroused by one more military invasion, they had far more fundamentally to embrace the enormous cost of the only realistic strategy by which a foreign power might diminish Taliban influence, namely, the effecting of serious economic reforms. U.S. policymakers seem to have imagined that more troops could counter the former, and that in spite of promising words to the contrary, they could safely ignore the latter. Yet it could never have been just a war on the Taliban; it had always to be a war on poverty.

However, from the beginning of the post-9/11 American intervention in Afghanistan (in the fall of 2001), that is, from the time the Americans used the warlords to conquer the Taliban and then chose Karzai to lead the nation, there was never any serious U.S. commitment to nation building, never any U.S.-led Marshall Plan for Afghan economic development—for good reason: the task is monstrous. Quite apart from the domestic limits set on American resources both by the earlier priorities of the Iraq war and by the later demands of the 2008 recession, the prospects for reconstituting Afghanistan's economy are awesomely out of reach. Only 12 percent of the land is arable. The population is largely illiterate. Corruption is widespread. Its economy lacks major sources of income other than opium. Its mineral resources have yet to be exploited. Its central government continues to rely on outside contributions. At bottom, significant economic reform would involve transforming a collection of competing medieval fiefdoms separated by history, culture, and language, into a cohesive economy with functioning, nationwide institutions, an outcome that took the countries of Europe perhaps five centuries to achieve.[5]

.   .   .   .   .

What do you do when you begin to realize that you have undertaken an impossible task, when you slowly begin to understand that there are no easy (read: military) solutions and that in fact your ambitions have far outstripped your resources? One option is to acknowledge your mistake and pull out. Another is to seek someone to blame.

In November of 2009, when President Obama was in the midst of an exhaustive review of his Afghan war policy, Karl Eikenberry, U.S. ambassador to Afghanistan, sent a secret analysis of his own to Hillary Clinton, U.S. secretary of state.[6] The military wanted a surge of forty thousand more troops. (Obama would eventually settle on thirty thousand.) Eikenberry wanted none, arguing that the need was for greater economic aid, not more troops. But how much aid?

Eikenberry's analysis reveals clearly the depth of American ambivalence about estimating accurately both the cost and the time required for a level of economic development sufficient to sideline the Taliban. At one point Eikenberry suggests the possibility of some success at modest expense:

> We should weigh whether a relatively small additional investment
> in programs for development and governance would yield results
> that, if not as visible as those from sending more troops, would
> move us closer to achieving our goals at far lesser cost and risk,
> both in lives and dollars.

At another point, however, he is far more candid about the enormous obstacles confronting adequate economic reform:

5. For parts of this paragraph, see Rashid, *Descent into Chaos*, 8, 133, 189–95, 329–30.

6. http://documents.nytimes.com/eikenberry-s-memos-on-the-strategy-in-afghanistan/.

> Beyond Karzai himself, there is no political ruling class that pro-
> vides an overarching national identity that transcends local affilia-
> tions and provides reliable partnership. Even if we could eradicate
> pervasive corruption, the country has few indigenous sources of
> revenue, few means to distribute services to its citizens, and most
> important, little or no political will or capacity to carry out basic
> tasks of governance.

Nowhere does Eikenberry evaluate the significant capabilities of the
indigenous Taliban to compete in the various areas of deficit he has just
outlined. Nowhere does he suggest that the U.S. may be failing because it
has undertaken an impossible task. Instead he seems to believe that one
isolated Afghan leader, chosen by the Americans, should be able, without
massive and prolonged U.S. investment, to overcome these deficits on his
own. Thus positioned, Eikenberry proceeds to blame Karzai.

> President Karzai is not an adequate strategic partner. The proposed
> counter-insurgency strategy assumes an Afghan political leader-
> ship that is both able to take responsibility and to exert sovereignty
> in the furtherance of our goal: a secure, peaceful, minimally self-
> sufficient Afghanistan hardened against transnational terrorist
> groups. Yet Karzai continues to shun responsibility for any sover-
> eign burden, whether defense, governance or development.

It is far easier to say, "You are inadequate," than to say, "I am inadequate—because I have set goals for you that are unattainable." Throughout
its long and fitful war effort, and with increasing pressure, the U.S. tried
to impose on Karzai expectations of its own that were wildly beyond realization. Karzai, president of Afghanistan (read: mayor of Kabul) was to
unite the warlords, eradicate corruption (read: the way the warlords have
always done business), and outcompete the Taliban—all the time lacking
the financial resources or a nationwide power base of his own other than
an army made up of impoverished recruits loyal to the extent they receive
international pay. With the Americans strenuously refusing to recognize
the impossibility of his achieving for them their goals, Karzai had to know
for some time that his patron had abandoned him.

Sowing the Seeds of Failure: The Manager

What happened that the vitally important trust between the parable's unequal but interdependent collaborators broke apart? This question, not

easily answered, is central to the parable's mystery. Could it also be that the manager, like President Karzai, has come to feel abandoned by his patron?

We begin with a prior question. Were the charges brought to the rich man that his manager was squandering his property true or false? If false, what silenced the manager's vigorous protest? If true, the parable listener is even more confounded.[7] Why would a competent estate manager, wholly dependent on his employer's goodwill for his security and even his survival, squander that goodwill? Other than the rich man's patronage, the manager possesses no separate resources, no alternative leverage to realize his own security. If he loses that patronage, he confronts, as he himself observes, the savage prospect of expulsion into the class of day laborers—that is, into a dramatically foreshortened life expectancy.

Puzzlement increases when the listener examines the charges more closely. The manager is not accused of using poor judgment or even of embezzling. (The narrative itself blocks any hypothesis involving simple incompetence; otherwise how can one account for the man's suddenly

7. Was the accusation against the manager that he squandered his master's property true or false? The Greek verb implicated here, *diáballō*, is complex. The Greek New Testament lexicographers Arndt and Gingrich in their *Lexicon*, 180 translate *diáballō* to mean "to bring charges with hostile intent, either falsely and slanderously . . . or justly." At issue is the distinction, within *diáballō* and within the fact of accusation, between intent (always malicious) and accuracy (sometimes accurate, sometimes not). In *diáballō*, therefore, clarity and ambiguity are intertwined.

Since the parable itself does not answer the question of whether the accusations are true or false, listeners are free to engage any of the three answers possible (true, false, or "don't know"). At issue in the interpreter's initial choice is the range of problems to be undertaken when attempting to create narrative consistency. Each pathway leads to different problems and thus to different readings. For example, Herzog assumes that the accusation is false. "[The Steward] is familiar with back-stabbing and has probably survived a few episodes of witch-hunting to reach his present position . . . In fact, the steward was just doing his job, and the charges brought against him are just a part of the endless war between the landowners and the peasants" (*Subversive Speech*, 245–46). Herzog is thereby obligated to explain why, if falsely accused, the shrewd, capable manager did not mount a vigorous defense. Here I choose to assume that the accusation is true. I am thereby obligated to explain why, if accurately accused, the shrewd, capable manager squandered his employer's property in the first place. Scott, *Hear Then the Parable*, 261–65, chooses to leave the question open. "Was the accusation of wasting goods true or false? . . . The parable offers no answers to these questions" (265). Scott is thereby obligated to engage neither of the above different sets of problems.

Perhaps the only criteria for judging among these three choices—a decision necessarily required of any listener prior to constructing some kind of consistency—is the coherence and richness of the reading each produces. Richness then becomes a function of what size and type of net one chooses to throw over the existing uncertainties; coherence, in turn, becomes more (or less) difficult to achieve—and more (or less) evocative.

reconstituted astuteness?) He is charged with squandering. The verb in Greek is *diaskorpidzō*. Its central idea is the scattering of seed or the dispersing of a flock of sheep, connoting an imprecision in planning or an inability to control an outcome. (Luke uses this same verb to describe the unthinking behavior of the Prodigal Son as he wastes his inheritance.) The manager is accused of wasting his lord's resources, throwing them to the winds, flushing them down the toilet. Examined from every angle, his behavior is incomprehensible. This man is shrewd. He has everything going for him. Then, through a seeming loss of control, he engineers his own disaster. What is going on?

I propose that the parable, subtlely, steadily, and inexorably, paints the listener into a corner. There is only one exit left. Listeners must look to the behavior of the rich man.

What Is One's Response to Being Utterly Dependent, Completely Burdened, and Steadfastly Ignored? (Karzai)

How do you feel when someone whose support you must have assigns you a difficult task, expects you to accomplish it, refuses to give you the resources to do so, and refuses to acknowledge that refusal? I suggest here that Karzai has experienced exactly this kind of bewildering conundrum, and I will suggest below that the manager has become equally enmeshed. Schematically there are perhaps three progressive stages in any response to such stress: (1) despair at being simultaneously dominated and completely dismissed, resulting in a flailing disorganization that appears to be incompetence but in reality is the consequence of being altogether deprived; (2) dawning realization that you are being abandoned, but well before you can see any alternative to shore up your ingrained dependency; and (3) discovering a real (or, tragically, imaginary) new person on whom you can depend and with whom you can collaborate. (In preparation, we can note the exquisite vulnerability of the subordinate as he or she enters stage 2; here the superior will capitalize on any hint of disaffection to impose an even more strident and more confident blaming.)

Ahmed Rashid, a Pakistani journalist who has known Karzai for almost two decades, met with him in November of 2010. Here he describes both his impressions and his analysis of the president's state of mind.

> Karzai . . . appears mistrusting of the West's long-term commitment to his country . . . Of late, he is convinced that the Americans

want to get rid of him . . . Last fall he reportedly told top U.S. officials that of the three "main enemies" he faced—the United States, the international community, and the Taliban—he would side first with the Taliban.[8]

From the Afghan president's perspective, Washington treats him with a mixture of insult and confusion . . . Throughout Afghan history, an ever present concern for political and physical survival has been an extremely important part of Afghan rulers' psyches . . . The same could be said of Karzai today. Handling a wary president preoccupied with keeping his own head requires a personal touch—something that Obama, for all his renewed commitment to the fight, sorely lacks . . . The U.S. president has been striking in his refusal—or inability—to get on with Karzai, never working to create the personal rapport the Afghan president enjoyed with his predecessor. It is Obama, not Bush, who has committed massive resources to Afghanistan while trying to improve the tattered U.S. reputation in the Muslim world. But Karzai still considers the Bush era a golden age for his presidency, a time when . . . [he] could pick up the phone any time and talk to the American leader.[9]

If we rely on Rashid's analysis, we can see that Karzai is here located in the second of the three stages outlined above. Still dependent on the U.S. and at the same time convinced he is being abandoned, he is deeply uncertain about finding new backers. He has no independent source of security, no warlord fiefdom of his own. While more and more openly critical of the U.S., he cannot break with his master, and the Americans, in turn, can find no one else to replace him. He is like a baseball player caught between bases.[10] As with a mutually dependent couple in a stable, unstable marriage, each keeps attacking the other, and each keeps making up. They have lost respect for each other and even hate each other—but they still need each other.

8. Karzai here threatens to engage with the same people who assassinated his father, Abdul Ahad Karzai, in July 1999.

9. Rashid, "How Obama Lost Karzai."

10. A former Taliban leader assessed Karzai's position as follows: "Karzai has very few friends who can help him to shoulder the burden . . . The way he came into power at the hands of foreign sponsors weakened his position from the very beginning. He has very few smart advisers who can give him clear, tough direction, in the light of Afghan culture. He . . . finds himself between the tiger and the precipice—he wakes up every day not knowing which way to go" (Zaeef, *My Life with the Taliban*, 222).

What Is One's Response to Being Utterly Dependent, Completely Burdened, and Steadfastly Ignored? (The Manager)

Something went terribly wrong between the rich man and his manager. Having scrutinized the manager's behavior and having come away even more puzzled, we turn to examine the behavior of the rich man. By looking closely at what this dominant figure does after the squandering, we can infer what most likely he had been doing before.

To summarize in advance: it would appear that the rich man's earlier attitude of valued collaboration with his manager had shifted, well before the parable begins, into one of arrogant aloofness and growing neglect. There are three clues supporting this hypothesis, none of them obvious.

The first clue pointing to the rich man's increasing indifference toward his manager is that he is unaware of how his subordinate has gone massively out of control; others have to tell him. The manager's flailing is flagrant; throwing property to the winds is not subtle. How is it that the rich man is himself ignorant? Was he physically absent? Or was he present but preoccupied and self-absorbed?

The second clue pointing to the rich man's indifference—and even arrogance—is that once he is informed of the wasting, he does not keep an open mind. With such an enormous amount of trust involved, one would think he would want to know the results of the audit before making any decision. If the charges are false, he should want to learn what caused the accusations. If the charges are true, he should want to understand what made his previously trustworthy subordinate destroy that trust. Even more, he should want to find out what in the first place led him to miscalculate so badly when judging the man's character. Instead, his reactions seem abrupt, even impulsive, and devoid of curiosity. "What is this that I hear about you? Give me an accounting of your management, because you cannot be my manager any longer." He treats this subordinate, with whom he has collaborated for so long, as a replaceable thing, not as a human being who has broken his trust. His language makes him appear as if he has already determined to discard their relationship—which is certainly what the manager believes.

Truly remarkable here is the rich man's inability to inquire into the charges, coupled with the manager's inability to explain himself to his lord; each has lost his earlier capacity to speak to the other. The silence, at this point in the narrative, is deafening. The manager's soliloquy and subsequent actions altogether miss the mark. His true target, the rich man, has disappeared. In what had been a relationship of great value to both men, silence has so overtaken speech that even the reasons for the speechlessness are buried in graves without markers.

The third clue pointing to the rich man's lack of interest in his manager's well-being is both more persuasive and more hidden: the rich man is so indifferent to how his highly dependent subordinate might actually feel about being dismissed that he fails to anticipate this vulnerable man's pressing need to betray. Thus, after firing him, the rich man foolishly leaves in his manager's hands the authority both to summon his wealthy debtors and to alter their contracts.

This clue, twice repeated, is muted in the text. It is first found inside the manager's rumination: "My master *is taking* the position away from me." The firing is not yet fully carried out. As the manager walks down the hall to get the books, he indeed believes he has been let go; however, as far as the debtors know, he is still in office. Lest listeners miss it, the manager repeats that fact: "*when* I am dismissed as manager." The manager's ability to command his master's wealthy debtors, each of whom owes the equivalent of tens of thousands of dollars, depends entirely on the debtors' belief that he remains vested with his employer's authority. Clearly the debtors would not have risked altering their contracts if they could not publicly assume (whether or not they privately suspected otherwise) that the manager was acting with the consent of the rich man. Had the man of wealth at once informed these important debtors of the dismissal, the debtors would not possibly have colluded with the manager, thereby imperiling the source of their needed loans.[11] But the manager's summons to the debtors outpaces any message to them from his lord.

Putting these clues together, I propose that what happened earlier between master and manager that resulted in the manager's inexplicable behavior of squandering was the manager's growing experience of being neglected. What this dependent manager lost, and what rendered him unable to function, was his certainty that his patron was still actively invested in his well-being. For someone so painfully dependent, it was as if the air was being sucked out of the room. Sensing that he has lost hold of the rich man's regard, he begins to experience profound doubt about his own security. As a result he feels depleted of the assurance undergirding his competence.

11. I owe most of the understandings in this paragraph to Bailey, *Poet and Peasant*, 98–99.

However, he cannot risk confronting his changed master. Since neither is able to speak to the other, the manager fills the emptiness with the speech of silence—that is, with a perplexing symptom. He squanders his patron's property; he scatters it with no concern about getting it back. Squandering suggests a sense of hopelessness, of a giving up, of a "What the hell! What does it matter anyway?" attitude. The manager's squandering represents in a disguised but precise manner what he experiences his patron as having done to him; the manager's scattering of property is in direct response to the rich man's scattering of care.

Central to his despair is the manager's inability to discover in the rich man any acknowledgment that he, the superior, might be responsible for the consequences of abandoning his subordinate. Hidden inside this end stage of collapse is an inarticulate, last-ditch hope. "Maybe, seeing me so radically changed, so inexplicably incompetent, my lord might wonder what is going on. Perhaps he might even say, 'I suspect something may be wrong; what could it be?'" But the rich man is altogether unable to discern in the manager's hurtful act the hidden message of appeal.

For whatever reason, the rich man behaves as if he finds out of reach the idea that he should be aware of, much less responsible for and responsive to, his manager's feelings. Instead he seems to assume that he should have a fully functioning subordinate without his needing to give him any serious attention, certainly not to the extent of having to imagine how he might feel, and most certainly not to the extent of having to retreat from his own privileged domination. Just as the Americans believe with Karzai, the rich man is convinced that his subordinate should fit into his own expectations—and never the other way around. (Look again at Ambassador Eikenberry's assessment: "[Karzai should] exert *sovereignty* in the furtherance of *our* goal" [italics added].[12])

As long as he kept hoping for the rich man's responsiveness, the manager was held suspended between a live possibility and despair. However, once the bond between the two is broken, once hope is gone, the manager is forced to look elsewhere for protection. Now he can at least begin to imagine that there might be others who would take him in. Despair is suddenly replaced by a reawakened hope—and thus a reconstituted shrewdness.

However, this new hope, from the outset, is doomed. It is illusory. It is erected upon a deception. The manager persuades himself that he will

12. http://documents.nytimes.com/eikenberry-s-memos-on-the-strategy-in-afghan-istan/.

secure the trust of new patrons through the betrayal of his present one. Yet his dishonesty cannot possibly provide him with the security he seeks. Not only, in his urgency, is he unconcerned about the harm he is doing to his employer; he is also, in his shrewdness, unaware of the damage he is doing to himself. Because the debtors have no access to the private distress motivating the earlier squandering, they lack the resources to decipher their later experience of the manager's dishonesty. While the debtors will for a time pay him off with favors, in the end no one will be taken in by taking him in. Who among them would entrust the management of his wealth to someone so prepared both to squander and to betray?

All the while the rich man deftly escapes blame. He praises his subordinate's behavior. He does so because to criticize him would be publicly to acknowledge his own stupidity in continuing in authority someone whom others had already recognized as out of control.[13] By commending his rogue manager, the lord covers up his own incompetence. Appearing generous, he avoids humiliation. Throughout the entire sequence he has been unable to hear what his manager, first dismissed from awareness, then dismissed in shame, and now dismissed with praise, has all along been trying to say.

As the community of his debtors and neighbors looks on, the rich man, forced to absorb large financial losses, now stands shamed—although no one dares say so. Not able to suspect his own participation, he exits feeling misused.

Neither man had been able to explore in words the private distress between them; neither thereby has been able to avoid these larger hurts, nurtured in silence, covered over with praise, and now flowing unimpeded into self-defeating consequences. The parable encompasses an intimate tragedy.

Epilogue

The war in Afghanistan has been most unusual. Our security could not be achieved by defeating our opponents; it could only be had by winning hearts and minds. We needed to gain the willing assent of vast numbers of

---

13. Here compare Bailey, *Poet and Peasant*, 101–2, who argues that by praising his subordinate, the master embodies before the entire community his own generous nature. The rich man chooses to "keep silent, accept the praise that is even now being showered on him, and allow the clever steward to ride high on the wave of popular enthusiasm . . . Because the master was indeed generous and merciful, he chose to pay the full price for his steward's salvation" (102).

Afghans. To the extent we destroyed bodies, to that extent we failed to win hearts and minds. We exercised our enormous military power in hopes of gaining control; in so doing we lost control. Jesus's parable explores precisely this dilemma, inviting its listeners, if they will, to discern another way.

The parable asks, "If you are someone powerful and you want someone less powerful to do something, how do you proceed?" The question is a universal one, good all the way from presidents down to parents. What you are seeking is willing collaboration, as the rich man sought when hiring his manager, and as we are after in Afghanistan.

When the powerful person respects his subordinate, the subordinate responds, "If you're in this with me and for me, I'll do everything I can for you." But if the powerful person says, "You must do what I want, but I am not obliged to discern what you want," then the battle for collaboration is lost. Then the subordinate responds, "If you're in this only for yourself and I'm just your tool, I'll fight you as hard as I can, whether I know what I'm doing or not, and even if it means my own collapse and possibly my own destruction."

Readers might say, "This chapter is far too complex; Jesus's parable cannot possibly contain all the meanings you ascribe to it."

I respond, "If you, the reader, dominate the parable by elevating the rich man and dismissing the manager, seeing the former simply as innocent and the latter simply as dishonest, then the parable will collapse on you and will become merely a puzzling and not very satisfying moral tale. But if you respect the parable—that is, if you look carefully into its hidden complexities, if you pay close attention to what does not make ready sense—then the parable will collaborate with you and will respond to you not only in the ways suggested above but also in other ways far richer—and far more disconcerting—than you ever expected."

A YOUNGER SON AND A FATHER

(The Prodigal Son)

THE SITUATION

There was a man who had two sons.

SCENE I

The younger of them said to his father, "Father give me the share of the property that will belong to me." So he divided his property between them.

SCENE II

A few days later the younger son gathered all he had and traveled to a distant country, and there he squandered his property in dissolute living. When he had spent everything, a severe famine took place throughout that country, and he began to be in need. So he went and hired himself out to one of the citizens of that country, who sent him to his fields to feed the pigs. He would gladly have filled himself with the pods that the pigs were eating; and no one gave him anything. But when he came to himself he said, "How may of my father's hired hands have bread enough and to spare, but here I am dying of hunger! I will get up and go to my father and I will say to him, 'Father I have sinned against heaven and before you; I am no longer worthy to be called your son; treat me like one of your hired hands.'" So he set off and went to his father.

SCENE III

But while he was still far off, his father saw him and was filled with compassion; he ran and put his arms around him and kissed him. The son said to him, "Father, I have sinned against heaven and before you; I am no longer worthy to be called your son." But the father said to his slaves, "Quickly, bring out a robe—the best one—and put it on him; put a ring on his finger and sandals on his feet. And get the fatted calf and kill it, and let us eat and celebrate; for this son of mine was dead and is alive again; he was lost and is found!" And they began to celebrate.

—Luke 15:11b–24 (NRSV)

8

A Younger Son and a Father: Waiting for God's Restoring or Restoring God's Waiting?

Why would a father, while still competent, surrender to his children control over his own economic future?

IT IS OFTEN SAID that those who search for the historical Jesus discover, reflected up from the bottom of the well, their own faces. This same potential for misapprehension increases markedly for interpreters of Jesus's parables. His complex metaphors are open to an array of possible understandings; little in their structure directly challenges the widespread tendency to find in them what one has learned to expect.

This reality of parable openness to listener expectation becomes especially germane when turning to these same narratives with the question of whether Jesus envisioned the imminent transformation of history. That is, did he anticipate the sudden intrusion into human experience of an externally imposed, unilateral, and (above all) conclusively final divine intervention? (Certainly John the Baptist, Paul, and the author of Mark's Gospel so imagined.) The question is central to any reconstruction of the historical Jesus; it focuses on how he conceived change to come about, both within history and within individuals. I propose the problem is illuminated by how we choose to understand Jesus's parable of the Prodigal Son.

The Parable and N. T. Wright

N. T. Wright, a major contemporary scholar of the historical Jesus, in his influential book, *Jesus and the Victory of God,* answers the question concerning divine intervention positively. The book's title implies his basic thesis: that through his own person Jesus believed God was about to restore, victoriously and within history, the fortunes of Israel. In supporting his position, Wright develops an interpretation of the Prodigal Son.

> Years of scholarship have produced many commentaries on Luke, and many books on the parables. But none that I have been able to consult has noted the feature which seems to me most striking and obvious. Consider: here is a son who goes off in disgrace into a far country and then comes back, only to find the welcome challenged by another son who has stayed put. The overtones are so strong that surely we cannot ignore them. This is the story of Israel, in particular of exile and restoration . . . The exodus itself is the ultimate backdrop: Israel goes off into a pagan country, becomes a slave, and then is brought back to her own land. But exile and restoration is the main theme. This is what the parable is about.[1]

Elsewhere Wright alludes to his overall strategy when approaching the question of the historical Jesus.

> The researcher, after a period of total and sometimes confusing immersion in the data, emerges with a hypothesis, a big picture of how everything fits together . . . [W]e can fill in this picture . . . in such a way as to draw in more and more of the evidence within a growing hypothesis about both Jesus himself and Christian origins . . . [T]he coherence and simplicity of the resulting picture, the sense that is made of the data, and the light that is shed on many other areas enable us to state with confidence that this, or something like it, is indeed how it was.[2]

Commenting on what he thought to be limits in Goethe's ability to evaluate Italian works of art, the Renaissance art historian Bernard Berenson observed, "We think in vain that we are free to look and see and appreciate everything on earth. Even the most gifted of us can never get much beyond what he was taught to appreciate in his formative years."[3]

---

1. Wright, *Victory*, 126. See also ibid., 51, 123–137, 242, 254–55, 267, 332, 395, 440, 533.

2. Borg and Wright, *Meaning of Jesus*, 22–23.

3. Berenson, *Passionate Sightseer*, 128.

When approaching Jesus's parables, we are all of us participants in Wright's methodology. We immerse ourselves in the data for longer or shorter periods of time and then emerge with a hypothesis, a big picture. Because we try to fit the remaining data into our already formulated big picture, we are all of us subject to Berenson's myopia. Perhaps the best we can do with the parables is listen carefully, create differing interpretations, and then invite judgments as to how well each renders coherent all that is available.

Irony in the Parable (Part 1)

Most studies of the Prodigal Son perceive the parable father as "all-good." To arrive at this conclusion, however, these same studies have had to ignore the implications of a vital question the story raises at the outset, namely, why would a father, while still competent, surrender to his children control over his own economic future? It would be a rare father in any culture at any time who would even consider behaving this way.[4]

We can widen the interpretive problem by including this troubling aspect of the father's behavior, or we can in the interests of discovering in the father's actions illustrations of divine intent, ignore it. By avoiding such exploration, we are free to continue perceiving the father as all-good. However, we are left endlessly wondering why Jesus saw fit in the first place to present his listeners with such a difficult problem. It is far easier to imagine a narrative in which the father, while continuing to reserve his universally acknowledged right to dispose of his assets at the time of his death, provides a substantial gift to an immature younger son intent on emigration. (Loss of such a gift would have consequences far less dire than loss of the inheritance.) Instead this story, if we choose to comprehend it more completely, lures us to ponder the implications of this father's peculiar behavior. He not only surrenders control over that portion of his estate destined for his younger son but simultaneously abandons his paternal prerogatives in relation to his undemanding elder son as well. Without evident reasons of his own, he determines prematurely to yield to his children the power to make decisions about his resources—that is, about his *bios* (literally, his "life").

It has been recognized for some time that hidden within the younger son's demand for control over his father's living is a wish that his father die.

4. That some in ancient Israel actually did so led, evidently, to the warning against the practice found in the apocryphal book of Sirach (33:19–24).

However, few have examined the ways the father's seeming collusion with that wish might undermine his son's still fragile maturing. Because their prior assumptions, supported by the parable's context in Luke, lead them to perceive in the father a figure for God, most commentators resist engaging this serious complication.[5]

By his inexplicable decision, provoked not by his own thoughtfulness but by his son's impetuosity, this seemingly generous father may be indirectly telling both his sons, "I have decided to surrender control over my own future—in the hope that thereby I can make you men." In response, his sons may indistinctly perceive that their father, by relinquishing such control while still capable, may have arrived at two profoundly disturbing conclusions: (1) "I do not expect, on my own and without you, to be able to complete my work"; and (2) "I do not expect that you, on your own and without me, will be able to complete yours." By including these realizations, some listeners may begin to discern the troubling possibility that this father's seeming generosity may not, in fact, be so generous; instead, his initiative may signal both a passive surrender of his own position in life along with a longing effort to determine the developing lives of his sons. The sons' contrasting responses (of careless collapse and of careful compliance) may in fact represent attempts—failed attempts for them both—to get out from under their father's need to be needed.

As the younger son leaves home, he feels himself entitled. Then, in that foreign land, he gradually discovers he possesses nothing of his own on which to build; instead, all he has is his father's imposition of an illusory competence. Slowly, and then more rapidly, he does a double-take. He is not full; he is empty. It is in this context that he destroys a patrimony so thoughtlessly imposed that he can only experience it as worthless. If his father insists on providing him with far too much far too soon, how can he begin to undertake his own risks, discover his own discipline, and rely on

5. A rare exception is Breech, *Silence*, chapter 12. In this groundbreaking work on the Prodigal Son, Breech was among the first to point out the profoundly complicating implications of the father's initial response. "The man's actions of dividing his living between his sons create a situation the significance of which must be clearly understood. In the thinking of the ancient world, questions regarding ownership of property and questions regarding father-son relationships were inextricable. What the man does—allowing himself to be treated as though dead and giving away his proprietary rights—is utterly unparalleled in any of the parabolic narratives which survive from antiquity (Jewish, Greek, or Latin). Since the situation is so extraordinary, the narrative raises the question of why the man, by dividing his living between his two sons, totally altered the basis of his relationship with them" (*Silence*, 190).

his own abilities? The elder son, through endless compliance, keeps on try-ing to compel a recognition of his independent competencies that his father is simply unable to provide. As traditional listeners to the Prodigal Son, we may find ourselves saluting in the father's behavior what in fact is a dis-guised controlling; and, at the same time, we may find ourselves demeaning in the sons' responses what in fact are forms of inadequate resistance.

I believe we need to suspect within this parable the presence of irony. Whole books have been written on the subject of irony.[6] It is perhaps as difficult to define as it is to comprehend. One inadequate, vague, but work-ing definition might be, *Things are not as they seem; more is going on than meets the eye.* In this particular parable, the father may not be as benign as he seems, and his sons may not be as blameworthy as they appear. This suspicion does not come easily. While we consider Jesus to be among the greatest of teachers, we remain reluctant to endow him with the detach-ment requisite for a creator of irony. "Such is the arrogance of us moderns," warns Bernard Brandon Scott, writing of Jesus' parables, "that we fail to recognize true complexity when it appears to us in unfamiliar forms."[7]

To heighten this possibility, we turn now to explore how Jesus in this parable may be mining equally complex ironies buried deeply inside his own tradition.

A Father and Two Sons: The Foundational Stories of Genesis

Wright is surely correct to relate the parable to the great master narratives of the Hebrew Bible. He focuses on the one that fits his major thesis, that of exile and restoration. But I think he needs to go further back, back to the foundational stories of Genesis. Much of the book of Genesis is built around accounts of a father and two sons: Abraham with Ishmael and Isaac; Isaac with Esau and Jacob, and Jacob with Joseph and his brothers. These narra-tives portray a parent standing atop a triangle and choosing the younger of two sons over the elder. Matriarchs and patriarchs, enacting God's desire while contravening God's law (see Deut 21:15–17), consistently give the inheritance, birthright, or paternal blessing to the younger son.

The inheritance in question signifies, among other things, the Land. These Genesis narratives, composed and fitted together by authors and edi-tors long after the events they purport to describe, retroactively sanction

6. For examples, see Muecke, *Irony and the Ironic*; and Booth, *Rhetoric of Irony*.

7. Scott, *Hear Then the Parable*, xi.

ancient Israel's dominance in Canaan.[8] God chooses the younger son (read: Israel) to receive the inheritance (read: the Land), and God denies the inheritance to the elder son (read: the competing tribes living in and around Canaan, represented by Edom, i.e., Esau). Sometimes Genesis makes this controlling metaphor explicit. "The Lord answered her, 'Two nations are in your womb, two separate peoples shall issue from your body; one people shall be mightier than the other, and the older shall serve the younger.'" (Gen 25:23) When, at the outset, the father agrees to divide the inheritance, the parable's early listeners would readily discern Jesus's allusion to these Genesis accounts of God dividing territory.

However, Genesis also interrogates this seemingly unambiguous sanctioning of domination. One important symbol deployed to indicate the presence of such questioning is the word "robe." Throughout Genesis, the word "robe" is the marker for being chosen; however, following its denoting of preference, "robe" also becomes the occasion for deception, loss, and enslavement.

．　．　．　．　．

After wresting the inheritance from his elder brother by disguising himself in Esau's robe, Jacob learns through painful experience how such usurpation can provoke life-threatening danger. Nonetheless, with amazing obtuseness, he determines later in life to bestow upon the adolescent Joseph a robe of special favor.[9] With this shortsighted giving Jacob revives the long-standing consequences of his earlier betraying, thereby sentencing his beloved Joseph to endure the same lethal jealousy that once so terrified him. With his unthinking generosity he provokes what he most fears: his cherished son's disappearance, apparent death, and actual enslavement. (Hard upon the parable father's similar generosity will follow precisely these same consequences.)

．　．　．　．　．

Listeners to the Jacob/Joseph saga are provided even more profound levels of irony. Across the transition from Genesis to Exodus, the theme of

8. See Davies, *Territorial Dimension*, 13.

9. Jacob's sons will later return this same robe to him, torn and bloodied, to deceive him who earlier, with a robe, was the one deceiving. See Alter, *Genesis*, 138–39, 214.

being chosen leading to downfall undergoes a massive transformation. No longer is degradation reserved simply for those siblings not chosen, like Esau, or for those chosen, like Joseph; it now becomes the fate of Israel itself. This last exclusion is the consequence of an earlier, magnificent inclusion. "Robe" (and its companion "ring"), which in the parable appear to be unambiguous evidences of the father's favor, derive directly from the parallel symbols used by Pharaoh to invest Joseph with power: his signet ring and robes of fine linen (Gen 41:42).

Yet these latter symbols, far from marking entrance into a stable belonging, instead anticipate the beginnings of a prolonged humiliation. The dramatic ending of the Joseph saga—and there is no better story in all literature—involving reconciliation among the brothers and the triumphal entry of Israel into Egypt, is finally rendered the distant foreshadowing of disaster. What appeared as a transfer of power from Pharaoh to Joseph is revealed as finite and failed. The bestowal of the father's robe and ring upon the privileged younger son now leads, as the book of Genesis closes and the book of Exodus opens, to Israel's descent into generations of Egyptian slavery—where no one gives them anything.

At the moment the father enfolds the returning prodigal in the best robe, suddenly stirred is this dormant array of Torah ironies hidden within what appears to be straightforward evidence of the father's benevolence. For Jacob to grasp the blessing, Esau must be betrayed. For Jacob to favor Joseph, the father is bereaved. Because Joseph is robed a prince, Israel becomes enslaved. If the father imposes the inheritance, his sons may fail to grow. What might Jesus be doing by lifting his narrative so deftly from within the strands of these anciently revered ambiguities?

Irony in the Parable (Part 2)

If the creators of the Jacob/Joseph saga pull listeners to suspect that the one primarily responsible for Joseph's enslavement is Jacob himself, could not these same authors be luring listeners to wonder about the relationship between God's gifting of the Land and Israel's later entitlement and eventual exile? If you are willing to recognize that the Genesis authors repeatedly grasped the irony of a caring parent with generosity endangering a chosen son, are you not invited to suspect that such troubling complicity might also be in the awareness of Jesus?

The present reading proposes that Jesus is building upon these deeply established Genesis ironies and that in so doing he is re-vising, looking again, at the Torah's exploration of the problems inherent in a parent's choosing one son over another. By employing the fraught biblical symbol of "robe," Jesus, I think, most clearly signals his own intent to be ironic; what the father hopes he is giving may be quite different from what the son believes he has received. Things may not be just . . . as they seem.

One place to look closely for this possible difference between father and son is to wonder about the son's response to his father's welcome. Because Wright identifies the father as a figure for God, he portrays the father's welcome as unambiguously healing and hopeful.

> Israel could be allowed to sin, to follow pagan idolatry, even to end up feeding the pigs for a pagan master, but Israel could not fall out of the covenant purposes of her god. She could say to her god 'I wish you were dead,' but this god would not respond in kind. When, therefore, Israel comes to her senses, and returns with all her heart, there is an astonishing, prodigal, lavish welcome waiting for her.[10]

However, because Wright identifies the father as a figure for God, he also misses any chance to suppose that a profound ambivalence may reside both within the father's advance and within his son's response. Does this father's passionate embrace in fact signal a consummate welcome? Or does it instead reveal the father's continuing inability to be a father? Is his shameless eagerness the evidence of a competent loving? Or could his rushing to offer a healing forgiveness instead represent a distressing denial of his insistent participation in his son's ongoing humiliation?

Thus Jesus's parable offers support for two widely divergent interpretations: (1) that the father's premature giving of the inheritance and his later forgiveness in fact provide successfully for both his sons; or, (2) that both the father's giving and forgiving are seriously flawed; his later forgiving serves to cover up his earlier participation in forestalling his children's growth. Wright, along with most interpreters, takes the former option. But what of the latter?

This road, less traveled, opens on to the possibility that the father's generous imposition has led to his younger son's envelopment in a precocious entitlement. However, somewhere inside himself the son knows that the resources now in his possession are not his. Hard upon this awareness

10. Wright, *Victory*, 129.

comes one even more devastating. He suspects that his father doubts his abilities on his own terms to become an adult. In despair, the son jettisons all that fostered his inaccurate privilege—because the premature giving has resulted in a disastrous aborting of his right to risk his own becoming.

With great subtlety, Jesus plays upon the irony lodged in this final sequence. As the destitute prodigal prepares his speech in anticipation of his shameful return, he lifts his words directly from the distraught lips of the most powerful man in the world. Battered by the eighth plague, "Pharaoh hurriedly summoned Moses and Aaron and said, 'I have sinned against the Lord your God and against you'" (Exod 10:16 NRSV).[11] As God draws the august Pharaoh to his knees, does not this father also draw his son into humiliation?

On his return home the son tries one last time to reestablish what has been lost. "Let me work for pay so that I can begin to restore the responsibility I must own in order to grow." But the father, gratifying a generosity born of his own need to be needed, cuts him off. The father's lavish welcome becomes a persuasive image of forgiveness only if one ignores these evidences of the father's ongoing collusion in his son's collapse.

Thus the parable introduces a reconciliation that can be understood as either fundamentally true or fundamentally false. Within this latter perspective, the underlying reasons for the son's destroying the patrimony have not been addressed. Alongside of "Father, I have sinned . . ." is also needed, "Son, I too have sinned; by giving you control over *my* work, I took away *your* right to make your own discoveries—as if I could do your work for you."

What Might Jesus Be Doing?

The second interpretive strategy outlined above supposes (1) that Jesus is being ironic, and (2) that in so doing he is engaging perhaps the central question of the Torah, namely, how does the God of some become the God of all? In this reading, the parable is portraying not how God in fact gives and forgives but rather how God is prevented from giving and forgiving because the parable's listeners have learned to believe in a god who divides the inheritance, that is, in a god who prefers some over others.

This challenge concerning the flaws in being chosen and being excluded, which Jesus may here be posing to his own Jewish tradition, is one

11. I owe awareness of the textual parallel to Bailey, *Jacob and the Prodigal*, 106.

addressed with equal potency to a Western Christendom that has inherited, prematurely, dominion over the earth. If we perceive a god who for our privilege and for our benefit divides the inheritance, the blessing, the earth, what then will follow? Jesus's parable offers us the inevitable consequences, namely, a faulty giving, a failed receiving, and an impotent forgiving.

What if we perceive our god to be choosing us over others, our nation over others? What if in so doing we give ourselves permission to ignore the plight of those we consider beyond the realm of God's desire? But does not God, the God of the universe, yearn to bless ancient Edom just as much as ancient Israel, modern Yemen just as much as modern America? What will be our fate if we in the United States believe in a god who must in some special way bless America? What if those of us who believe ourselves thus chosen move from understanding ourselves gifted and therefore responsible to all the world to assuming ourselves entitled and therefore sanctioned to take from all the world?

If we worship a god prepared to give us, and only us, far too much far too soon, are we not then tempted to spend our gifted resources profligately, without thought either for others or for the future? For example, in today's world, under an assumed aegis of divinely sanctioned privilege, we claim an inordinate share of the earth's oil, consume it thoughtlessly, and with abandon pump its carbon into the atmosphere. At some point will not reality return that atmosphere back to us—torn and bloodied like Joseph's robe of special favor—to scorch our cities, flood our coasts, exacerbate our storms, and expand our deserts? After such a humiliating, devastating famine, shall we then be enveloped in God's robe of forgiveness? Or will it turn out to be merely the compromised robe of denial that from the outset has been all that our prodigal god would ever be able to provide?

How then does the god of some become the God of all? How does the god who divides on behalf of some become the God who provides on behalf of all—with the necessary corollary that the resources of the earth, divinely provided, belong equally to all? Does not the answer proceed from within the fundamental decision Jesus's parable offers us, namely, which kind of father do we choose to perceive, and which kind of God do we choose to worship?

Jesus's Vision of the Kingdom of God

If one entertains the possibility that what appears in his parable to be God forgiving may in fact be something far different, then another perspective is added to the debate about whether Jesus anticipated the sudden intrusion into human experience of an externally imposed, unilateral, and (above all) conclusively final divine intervention into human history.

If Jesus can properly be described as luring his audience into awareness through a difficult-to-discern irony, then the strategy he is adopting is about as distant as can be imagined from any straightforward proclaiming of God's unilateral and complete transforming of history. Whether we anticipate it or not, God's externally imposed victory will confront us inexorably. Irony, by contrast, remains endlessly in the shadows, open to discovery only if we work to seek it out. Whatever constitutes irony, it does not come upon us victoriously.

· · · · ·

Wright warns against reducing Jesus's words to "timeless truths," thereby stripping away their intense anticipation and compelling urgency. But, one needs to ask, does Jesus's urgency necessarily imply, as it does for Wright, the expectation of a "climactic" and "decisive" victory?[12] Or does Jesus's capacity for irony suggest a more mutually shared, less finally complete, but still impinging expectation of change? Such an alternative involves shifting away from the idea of an all-encompassing, catastrophically beautiful fulfillment. It means turning toward an understanding of how the coming of God's kingdom or God's rule or God's desire for the earth involves an open-ended beckoning, a noncoercive set of invitations that nonetheless contain a similar infusion of urgency and hope. Should one choose to suppose Jesus's irony, then it is possible to discern in his parable not the coming of God's powerful victory but rather the presence of God's profound yearning. For the historical Jesus, it may be that God's restoring is revealed, paradoxically, in God's waiting.

12. Borg and Wright, *Meaning of Jesus*, 35.

THE POOR AND A HOUSEHOLDER

(The Great Banquet)

THE SITUATION

Someone gave a great dinner and invited many.

SCENE I

At the time for the dinner he sent his slave to say to those who had been invited "Come, for everything is ready now."

SCENE II

But they all alike began to make excuses. The first said to him, "I have bought a piece of land, and I must go out and see it; please accept my regrets." Another said, "I have bought five yoke of oxen, and I am going to try them out; please accept my regrets." Another said, "I have just been married, and therefore I cannot come."[1] So the slave returned and reported this to his master.

SCENE III

Then the owner of the house became angry and said to his slave, "Go out at once into the streets and lanes of the town and bring in the poor, the crippled, the blind, and the lame." And the slave said, "Sir, what you ordered has been done, and there is still room." Then the master said to the slave, "Go out into the roads and lanes, and compel people to come in, so that my house may be filled."

—Luke 14:16b–23 (NRSV)

1. A source for the excuses in the parable, especially for the version in Thomas 64, may have been Deut 20:5–7, where a priest is addressing troops preparing for battle. "Has anyone built a new house . . . ? He should go . . . Has anyone planted a vineyard . . . ? He should go . . . Has anyone become engaged to a woman and not yet married her . . . ? He should go . . ."

106

9

The Poor and a Householder,
the Third World and Debt

Can the householder regain honor by commanding others?
Can he sustain generosity in the face of anger?
Can he evoke respect without relinquishing control?

A MAJOR HYPOTHESIS PURSUED in this book proposes that many of Jesus's longer parables may be understood in two differing directions at the same time. Such potential arises because these stories enclose two separate points of view, that of a superior character and that of his subordinate(s).

The listener is called upon to keep *both* in awareness. The present chapter seeks to challenge the segregation of perspectives that pervades our usual understanding of Jesus's parable of the Great Banquet.

Two Differing Interpretations:

In his 1998 book, *The God of Jesus,* Stephen J. Patterson presents two differing interpretations of this parable. This chapter came into being through the stimulation of Patterson's important work; it seeks to develop further some of the implications of his second interpretation.

Patterson's first interpretation represents the prevalent understanding of this narrative.

> The parable exemplifies the breathtaking generosity of God. So what does it mean to call Jesus "Christ" or "Messiah"? It is to proclaim that with Jesus the reign of God was here, that it was and is just as he described it. But can we believe that this is true? Can we believe that the reign of God is like a banquet in which the blind, the poor, and the lame find a place? Can we believe that God will welcome into it anyone who dares to come in? That is what it means to call Jesus the Christ. It is to accept his vision of the banquet and the God who comes with it."[2]

Patterson expands this interpretation.

> The peculiar and challenging thing about this parable is just this: the doors to the banquet hall are to be thrown wide open. "Go out to the highways and bring in whomever you might find there." Men and women. Friend and foe. The clean and unclean, Jews and Gentiles. Princes and thieves. Anyone who dares to respond to the invitation may come inside.[3]

By contrast, Patterson's second interpretation concentrates on dilemmas aroused within the donor. It starts with a distinction in social ranking. The householder is a member of a class of well-off people who, unlike the poor, are immersed in a culture of honor and shame. For them, "honor and shame are two of the basic anthropological dimensions of ancient life."[4] If his banquet invitation is accepted, the householder is honored; if it is rejected, he is shamed.

> To have honor is to have a place, a role, within which one is readily recognized by one's peers . . . Acquiring honor involves three basic steps. First, you must aspire to a role, a place in your culture. Second, your peers must recognize you in that role. Finally, once you are recognized in a role, you must now be able successfully to function in that role. If all of this falls into place, you acquire a grant of honor. However, if at any point the process breaks down, you are shamed.[5]

Here Patterson moves away from emphasizing the householder's remarkable inclusion of the marginal and instead focuses on the difficulties he is having in including himself. In this reading the story begins with

2. Patterson, *God of Jesus*, 49.

3. Ibid. 86.

4. Ibid., 73.

5. Ibid., 74.

the householder feeling humiliated. He has now to recover what has been abruptly wrested from him, namely, his honor, his public reputation, his standing in the community.

Can the Householder Regain Honor by Commanding Others?

At the center of Patterson's second, less explicit but intriguing understanding are the ambiguities lodged within the householder's subsequent actions. Blended inside his generosity is the problem of recovering his honor. Listeners must work to distinguish these two dimensions. One starting place is to ponder the householder's reaction to having been humiliated. According to Luke's version, he becomes angry.[6]

Given how involved he is in a social context so completely focused on issues of honor and shame, the householder's anger makes ready sense. This prominent personage says, "I extended myself. I not only offered you hospitality, I exposed my honor. By rejecting my invitation, you disrespected me. I feel humiliated. And I feel angry."

If we assume that his anger is evidence of a wounded self-esteem, then the householder is responding as if those who have declined his invitation have taken something from him. However, hidden inside this reaction is the irony that *he* is the one who long ago ceded to others the power to humiliate him. In the honor/shame culture of the householder, honor is traded like a commodity. What you have to do to be "honorable" is prescribed. Mutual respect among peers is maintained through the reciprocal give-and-take of carefully defined obligations. However, in exchange for the security of such mandated reciprocities, the householder has had to surrender to his peers the authority to determine his place.

As he confronts this sudden loss of respect, the householder has open to him a range of options. But he can see only one. He must restore his

---

6. We can observe the wide range of intensity assigned to the householder's anger in the three extant versions of this parable. In order to make the anger fit his allegorical reading, Matthew wildly exaggerates it. "the rest [of the original invitees] seized his slaves, mistreated them, and killed them. The king was enraged. He sent his troops, destroyed those murderers, and burned their city" (Matt 22:6b–7, NRSV). Thomas, by contrast, minimizes that same anger into nonexistence. "The slave returned and said to his master, 'Those whom you invited to dinner have asked to be excused.' The master said to his slave, 'Go out into the streets and bring back whomever you find to have dinner.'" (Thomas 64:10–11, Scholar's Version). Luke takes a middle ground: "Then the owner of the house became angry" (Luke 14:21, NRSV).

honor *by himself and on his own terms.* Resolving to avoid being humiliated a second time, he turns to people he knows will be unable to reject him. He is indeed being generous, and everyone will salute him for it. However, under the guise of charity, he is retreating into relying on the security of his economic position.

The parable raises the following question: by inviting the poor to become substitutes for his rejecting guests, will the householder in fact be able to recover respect? The vulnerability of his strategy is at the center of the present reading. The manner in which his inviting is overtaken by his demanding suggests his uncertainty. "Compel people to come in!" His self-doubt has reason. What kind of edifice for the resolution of his shame can this man erect on his unilateral effort to control? By relying on his economic position, can he truly overcome his humiliation at being disrespected? Or will his determination to remain in control defeat him?

Ironically, the householder may be discovered as having used his power to evoke a response that, were it to be meaningful, would (1) have to come from his equals, and (2) have to come voluntarily. Instead, he has chosen to command persons who, because of their weak position, have no alternative but to comply. Precisely because they lack independence, these people can be of no use in resolving what has caused his shame in the first place, namely, loss of regard from his equals.

Here is exposed the vulnerable underbelly of the magnificent generosity so emphasized in the parable. Nothing is wrong with it and everything is wrong with it. By trying to erase his shame unilaterally, the householder is avoiding having to depend on the freely given responses of others. *He* himself would never submit to being coerced. *He* would demand recognition across equality. *He* would expect to have been truly invited—which means he would want and require the right to refuse.

Can the Householder Sustain Generosity in the Face of Anger?

The householder has filled his house with the destitute. He has thereby erected a fragile bridge across the great gulf separating the poor from the well-off. His strategy—to use generosity across inequality to evoke respect—now faces predictable, if unanticipated, challenges. If his banquet is merely a single, one-off occasion, he is in no difficulty. But what will happen if he *keeps on* bringing together what society insists on keeping separate?

He would then be gradually exposed to the feelings of those receiving his generosity. At the outset the destitute cannot conceive of being angered by the great man's unquestioned assumption that they have no choice but to submit. For such persons this wealthy man's house is no more an occasion for shame than a garbage dump; all they know is how hungry they are. Likewise, most passersby live outside the householder's preoccupation with social standing. Both the poor and those who pass by have little interest in attaining positions of honor. To experience social shaming, one must first aspire to a place within the social hierarchy.[7]

However, not to feel anger does not mean not to have anger. The disrespect the householder has experienced for a moment—and to which he reacts with such intensity—is a humiliation the destitute have known all their lives. In the way a frozen foot thaws, where warmth produces pain, the householder's generosity, if continued, will inevitably release in his beneficiaries newly awakened resentment.

What would be the stages whereby the destitute might experience and then express their rage at having been so thoroughly excluded? Along with the householder, listeners must work hard to imagine the gradual unfolding of feelings inside persons so profoundly marginalized that they no longer have access to their fury. Initially, the poor may appear grateful and may even feel grateful. These exceedingly deprived persons will have to go through a lengthy process in order to achieve enough self-respect even to consider resisting the householder's unintended arrogance. They have yet even to conceive of responding, "You can't just *expect* me come. You have to show *respect*. You have to *invite* me. Then you have to *wait*. *I* get to choose whether I will come or not." The householder, of course, already has such retorts at his fingertips. His facility here illustrates how, should he choose to go towards the poor, the terrain he must cross will be as hard to win as the terrain the poor must cross in order to reach him.

Eventually such suppressed responses will come into open conflict with those needed to sustain a social honoring. Then it will not simply be, "We, the destitute, will continue to be grateful to you, our benefactor." It will rather be, "If you, our benefactor, maintain your giving long enough for us to find our voice, that voice will not be easy to hear."

At this stage the householder is unable to anticipate these coming reactions. He is still trying to cope with his own wounded feelings. However, given the likely advent of such disorienting responses, will he be able to

7. Ibid., 74.

maintain his remarkable initiative? Or will he, like the vineyard owner, be revealed as having created merely an *appearance* of generosity? The question remains open.

Can the Householder Evoke Respect without Relinquishing Control?

While earlier the gift of respect was possessed by the householder's erstwhile invitees, it now resides with his actual guests. He can compel from them an outward compliance, but he cannot coerce from them what he so much desires, namely, an inward respect. In this matter of overcoming shame, he must now rely on the unencumbered response of a group of persons who are not his equal. To garner such regard, he is being lured, however imperceptibly, to seek greater equality with these strangers. In order to gain access to the only place where true respect can develop, namely, the domain of interdependent equality, the householder will have to relax the unilateral assumption of gracious power that has for so long invaded his initiative.

There is more. Beyond having to sustain his initiative in the face of awakened anger, and beyond having to relinquish the security of control through generosity, a further disconcerting discovery awaits the householder. In brief, can he in fact enliven in the destitute respect towards himself by relying on resources that the poor, when they become able to think about it, will realize he has long ago stolen from them? In the agrarian economies of the ancient world, for the rich to have more means the poor must have less.

The Problem of Third World Debt

Here is where the householder's dilemmas merge with our own. Here is where the parable interacts with a major contemporary example of the rich stealing from the poor, namely, the problem of Third World debt. Originating in the last quarter of the twentieth century, this problem has swept into the twenty-first nearly unimpeded and almost completely ignored. For complicated reasons, a privileged minority of First World financial lenders has gained control over the economic resources of a vast number of the world's poor. Because many midlevel and poor countries have come to owe more money to these First World bankers than they receive from the largess of First World governments, less and less money remains in the hands of common people. The rich are rendering the poor even poorer. This hemorrhaging seems impossible to staunch.

How the Third World (meaning the earth's poorest and least developed countries) has come to be paying the First World (meaning the earth's richest and most developed nations) more in debt service than it earns in commerce or receives in aid may be outlined in three stages, with the third stage (working toward debt relief) still being tortuously debated.

(1) Over the last three decades of the last century, the First World and the Third World, acting in concert, created what for the Third World has become an impossibly huge debt, now to a large extent made up of interest payments due on loans (rather than the loans themselves). In 1973, partly in response to United States support of Israel during the Arab-Israeli Yom Kippur War, the Organization of Arab Oil Producing Countries imposed an oil embargo on the United States. The resulting sharp reduction in the available supply of oil soon led to spikes in its price, which in turn produced huge surpluses of capital seeking investment. In response, private banks in Japan, the U.S., and Europe rapidly increased the loans they were making to both the private and public sectors in developing countries. At that time interest rates were low. Given these conditions of excess capital and low interest rates, First World bankers frequently contracted loans without careful investigation of their potential profitability. Many of these loans turned out to be "nonperforming," that is, unable to realize a sufficient profit. Responsibility for the ongoing liabilities soon reverted to Third World governments. So began the repayment problem.

(2) At the end of the 1970s and the beginning of the 1980s, two debilitating events, both beyond their control, seriously compromised the ability of Third World governments to repay. The variable interest rates charged on their loans rose, and the price of the export commodities (for example, copper, bauxite, coffee), with which the Third World nations were to pay off their debt, fell. Using as leverage the need in the Third World for more money in order to remain credit worthy, First World bankers began imposing conditions on the provision of new loans (to be used largely to pay back to these same bankers the inflated interest on earlier loans). This leverage effectively gave First world bankers major control over Third World economies. To a significant extent—and for far into the foreseeable future—the economic policies of the Third World have had to submit to the directives of intermediary institutions (particularly the International Monetary Fund [IMF] and the World Bank) that are under the control of financial interests

in the First World. These interests, through these intermediaries, continue to require Third World governments to adopt austerity policies that divert resources away from domestic priorities in order to earn the foreign exchange needed to service their debt—that is, in order to ensure the continued flow of money from poor countries to rich countries. Believing that the debtor nations alone should be held responsible for the consequences of their borrowing, the First World imposed strategies that placed the repayment of burgeoning interest ahead of programs that might address the Third World's most pressing needs.

(3) The original, radical divide within the Third World between those who received the benefits of borrowing and those who eventually had to pay its costs fitted all too well with the often reckless lending practices of First World bankers. While Third World entrepreneurs and governments, frequently motivated by their own short-term interests, were the ones who both took out the loans and most often profited from them, the burden of having to repay them fell—and continues to fall—on the shoulders of the entire population, especially the poor. Before these poor can focus on helping themselves and their children, they must first pay off massive amounts of interest accruing on loans taken out by others long ago. Thus, toward the end of the last century, a debate intensified as to whether responsibility for the debt problem should fall solely on the debtors who initially made irresponsible *borrowing* decisions, or whether the debt problem should also be shared with the creditors who initially made irresponsible *lending* decisions. This debate has continued, unresolved, into the present. Still unanswered is the question, should the creditor nations provide significant debt relief, or should they continue to require the debtor nations to pay unsustainable levels of interest?[8]

. . . . .

Apportioning responsibility for this intractable problem is exceedingly difficult. No one questions the right of First World bankers to charge interest on their loans. But somehow millions of Latin American, African, and Asian poor people, for their lifetimes and the lifetimes of their children, have been required to pay to the rich of the industrialized nations

8. The above brief description of the history of this problem reduces its complexity while omitting significant additional factors that have contributed to Third World poverty. In developing this description, I have relied largely on Woodward. *Debt, Adjustment and Poverty;* see especially 15–31, 44, 68, 72–75, and 101–3.

enormous sums of money that they can in no way afford. In scope and depth—though not in planned malevolence—this form of economic imperialism easily matches anything conceived of by ancient aristocrats.

The Analogue between the Parable and Third World Debt

In order to entertain any analogy between the parable and this global event, readers must move between two widely different domains employing widely contrasting vocabularies: (1) the parable's difficulties in maintaining empathy between unequal persons, and (2) the indebted countries' difficulties in overcoming barriers thrown up by market forces. In the second instance, the impersonal structures of modern economies make its protagonists inured to the felt experience of vast numbers of Third World citizens. Would I do to my own child what the International Monetary Fund's policies do to a Third World child? Never! But the IMF administrator, of course, is far more insulated from that Third World child's experience than I am from my own child's pain. Nonetheless, what can be described as impersonal is, at bottom, still the result of human decision-making, however distant and however disguised.

Western bankers and financial institutions may focus on the obligation of poorer countries to repay their interest on loans no matter how they were incurred, but then First World citizens can no longer assume that their countries' generous aid will evoke respect. Are we in fact helping these poorer countries, as we would like to believe, or are we on balance harming them? In the parable's terms, can the householder overcome with his charity the long-standing inequities embedded in his economic dominance?

Woodward believes that "the responsibility for resolving the debt crisis lies squarely with the creditor governments: they alone can act to reform the international financial system; and only by such reform can the crisis be resolved."[9] Such a resolution would involve present creditors taking responsibility for bad lending decisions made by their forebears forty years ago. Instead, creditors continue to demand that present debtors take responsibility for borrowing decisions made by *their* forebears forty years ago. The aroused voices of the poor, seeking debt relief in Latin America in the 1980s, challenged such entitlement with the slogan, "Justice, not charity!"

9. Ibid., 146. See also 148–49 and 171–74.

The Work of Parable Listeners

Readers may experience this chapter's unearthing of potential complications as undermining the parable's straightforward allusion to God's all-embracing provision. There is no way definitively to adjudicate this tension. The parable allows *both* for straightforwardness *and* for complexity.

By crossing a major boundary in search of his honor, the householder has positioned himself to penetrate further boundaries. He could turn aside from this opportunity. He could simply dismiss his guests once the dinner is over—and with them their lifetimes of experience. Or, by continuing his contact, he could enter with them more profoundly into that same alien experience. The choice is up to him.

Listeners to the parable are confronted with precisely this same choice.

If listeners choose to perceive in the householder a figure for God, they can then turn aside from any further effort to empathize with the dispossessed. God's sustaining provision will embrace and overcome the entire skein of difficulties outlined above. Such listeners are thereby free to rejoice—but not to sweat.

By contrast, if listeners understand their work to mean that they are to *embody* the longing of God, their participation in God's empathy will of necessity encounter complications. By rubbing shoulders with his second set of invitees, by smelling their dirt, the householder, and listeners with him, has come upon a chance to break apart long-established barriers. But what will happen when the householder's continued responsiveness enlivens the long silenced resentment of the dispossessed? Even worse, what will happen when the householder's continued responsiveness arouses the dormant resistance of the powerful? God's love for the whole world comes into inevitable conflict with the possessive love of a minuscule portion of humanity for that tiny part of creation they believe they can control. The householder has arrived at the edges of this conflict. Listeners are beckoned to enter it. Jesus's whole way of living and the manner of his execution deeply engage it. What changes would then have to occur in the householder, and in us, for him to be able to sustain his remarkable initiative?

The coming work will require an increased awareness. By empathizing with the experience of those we have helped to dispossess, we begin to see how the their released anger toward us is a mirroring of the violence we have long imposed. Such awareness strengthens our ability to engage the resentment that will surely follow any newly awakened self-regard.

The coming work will also require an increased resilience. Lying in wait behind the question, "What is your part in getting us poor into your house?" is an earlier question, "What is your part in getting us poor?" The householder and ourselves with him are now drawn to loosen reliance on our initiative and instead to query our prior obligations. By becoming more deeply aware of the effects of our own control, we begin to render the deprived other more of an equal. However, by breaking open these long-established barriers to equality, we will be arousing the intense animosity of the privileged.

Finally, the coming work will require an increased reliance on others. Listeners begin to recognize that what the householder shies away from is what we all avoid, namely, a growing understanding that the only way out of being disrespected is the risky strategy of relying on the freely given response of others. Unlike the certain securities endemic to the world of honor and shame, this fragile equality has a far greater chance of evoking precisely that trustworthy regard for which we have for so long been seeking.

We have now reached the point of joining together the two strands of this interpretation: (1) the householder's need, and our own, for freely given respect, and (2) the releasing of others from our control, thereby allowing them to give us the very respect we seek. These two strands interact with and nurture each other. However, given the awesome extent of the householder's (and our own) coming work, they require a third term.

This third term involves recognizing God's essential provision *both* to the dispossessed *and* to the provider. The householder's embracing of God's provision is foundational to any successful provision of his own. In this way of understanding, the parable's promise of provision returns, but this time to succor a battle-weary householder.

What the householder needs, as do we all, is not only to give but also to receive: to take in the all-important reality that he too *already has* a place in God's eyes. The reciprocity of obligation, the requirement to pay back what one has been given, so essential to a society based on honor and shame, is now without purchase. One can receive without having to give. One can give without having to receive.

Imbibing that respect while kneeling in the presence of the God of Jesus in turn stimulates a transforming discovery: that the poor, the stranger, the unknown other, also have a place in God's eyes. Accepting that we are held by God merges with recognizing how others, all others, are also held by God. Here is an essential resource for discovering equality across difference.

If we take in the regard of God, we are empowered to supply that same regard to others. They in turn grow in their capacity to reciprocate. In global terms, we realize we cannot win by only taking. We can win only if we also give. Engaged in such a maturing process of more freely giving and more freely taking, we may at some point realize we have entered the kingdom of God.

A WIDOW AND A JUDGE

(The Unjust Judge)

THE SITUATION

In a certain city there was a judge
who neither feared God
nor had respect for people.

SCENE I

In that city there was a widow
who kept coming to him and saying,
"Grant me justice against my opponent."

SCENE II

For a while he refused,

SCENE III

but later he said to himself,
"Though I have no fear of God
and no respect for anyone,
yet because this widow keeps bothering me,
I will grant her justice,
so that she may not wear me out
by continually coming."

—Luke 18: 2b–5 (NSRV)

10

A Widow and a Judge,
Climate Change and Fossil-Fuel Executives

Why would a judge, having devoted his life to achieving a public office essential to fostering his community's cohesion, so completely reject that heritage?

As THEY HAVE BEEN remembered, Jesus's longer parables invariably present complex interactions compressed within condensed narratives. The parable of the Unjust Judge carries this combination to an extreme. With deft strokes, Jesus seals together in one closed container the utmost of his culture's experience of power and impotence. Entwined for a brief moment are hugely different worlds, almost always separated. Crucially, the parable allows no third person, no law, to enter and influence what either of these two protagonists is able to do.

Within this metaphor of two people locked together in an enclosed space with no one else positioned to intervene, this judge has all the power. The widow cannot appeal his decision. No one can overrule what he decides. This eminent jurist, who should be in the forefront of submission to law, revels in his capacity to subvert law. The widow, deprived of law, has nowhere else to turn. It should be impossible to come upon this story and not want to change it.

The world is confronting the imminent danger of global warming. Although the reality of this approaching disaster is now well established, corporate and political self-interest, enabled by a culture of consumer-driven apathy, is overwhelming a widespread scientific consensus with wave after wave of denial. The judge believes he can successfully ignore the law of God; fossil fuel magnates believe they can successfully ignore the laws of physics. Their lack of respect for the Earth's limits is about to bring crashing down upon us—and upon generations to follow for tens or even hundreds of thousands of years—massive dislocation and destruction. It should be impossible to come upon this story and not want to change it.[1]

How What Should Be Connected Has Become Disconnected: The Judge

After going into a city and identifying a judge, the parable reveals what the judge would never acknowledge openly. This man "neither feared God nor had respect for people."

These are astonishing claims. By definition, a judge cannot decide disputes by himself but is instead charged with interpreting his community's intention. In the Judaic culture of the parable, this intention is lodged in the Torah's exposition of the covenant relationship established between God and his people. The covenant was a mutual agreement, a commitment by God to his people reciprocally claiming a commitment from the people to God. The entire foundation of ancient Judaism, all of its jurisprudence and all of its polity, was built on allegiance to this shared commitment.

In his farewell address to all Israel, Moses declares,

> See, I set before you this day life and prosperity, death and adversity. For I command you this day, to love the Lord your God, to walk in His ways, and to keep His commandments, His laws, and His rules, that you may thrive . . . But if your heart turns away and you give no heed . . . I declare to you this day that you shall certainly perish . . . I have put before you life and death, blessing and curse. Choose life. (Deut 30:15–19, Tanakh)

The judge chooses comfort and curse. He claims commitment to no one—certainly not to God. His retreat into self-sufficiency disdains a

---

1. See Stager, *Deep Future*, 10: "We face a simple choice in the coming century . . . either we'll switch to nonfossil fuels as soon as possible, or we'll burn through our remaining reserves and then be forced to switch later on. In either case, greenhouse gas concentrations will probably peak some time before 2400 AD and then level off . . . [T]he global warming trend will top out and then flip to a long-term cooling recovery . . . But that process will last for *tens or even hundreds of thousands of years*."

mutuality that undergirds an entire culture. This arrogant man simply takes the entire deeply established ancient edifice of the covenant and drops it into the sea.

The judge needs also to boast of his contempt for others; he avows he has "no respect for anyone." Behind his facade of commitment to law, this nonjudge does not choose among alternatives while remaining prepared to change his point of view. Instead, he manifests an all-encompassing rejection of any influence. With suspect conviction, he locates himself inside his imaginative world as an extreme individualist. He is proposing that he belongs to no community, that he is dependent on no one and obligated to no one. Ultimately, he is claiming to be self-originating.[2]

How What Should Be Connected Has Become Disconnected: Fossil-Fuel Executives

Below are a series of quotes from the November 2014 Synthesis Report of the United Nations Intergovernmental Panel on Climate Change.

> Human influence on the climate system is clear, and recent anthropogenic emissions of greenhouse gases are the highest in history. Recent climate changes have had widespread impacts on human and natural systems.
>
> Warming of the climate system is unequivocal, and since the 1950s, many of the observed changes are unprecedented over decades to millennia. The atmosphere and ocean have warmed, the amounts of snow and ice have diminished, and sea level has risen.
>
> Anthropogenic greenhouse gas emissions have increased since the pre-industrial era, driven largely by economic and population growth, and are now higher than ever. This has led to atmospheric concentrations of carbon dioxide, methane and nitrous oxide that are unprecedented in at least the last 800,000 years. Their effects . . . are extremely likely to have been the dominant cause of the observed warming since the mid-20th century.
>
> Continued emission of greenhouse gases will cause further warming and long-lasting changes in all components of the climate system, increasing the likelihood of severe, pervasive and irreversible impacts for people and ecosystems.
>
> Surface temperature is projected to rise over the 21st century under all assessed emission scenarios. It is very likely that heat

2. For the previous two sentences, I am indebted to Roy Schafer, "Conformity and Individualism," in Shapiro, ed., *Inner World and the Outer World,* chapter 2.

waves will occur more often and last longer, and that extreme precipitation events will become more intense and frequent in many regions. The ocean will continue to warm and acidify, and global mean sea level to rise.

Climate change will amplify existing risks and create new risks for natural and human systems. Risks are unevenly distributed and are generally greater for disadvantaged people and communities in countries at all levels of development.

Many aspects of climate change and associated impacts will continue for centuries, even if anthropogenic emissions of greenhouse gases are stopped. The risks of abrupt or irreversible changes increase as the magnitude of the warming increases.

Without additional mitigation efforts beyond those in place today, and even with adaptation, warming by the end of the 21st century will lead to high to very high risk of severe, widespread, and irreversible impacts globally (high confidence).[3]

3. Intergovernmental Panel on Climate Change, *Climate Change 2014: Synthesis Report*, http://www.ipcc.ch/report/ar5/syr/.

What follows is excerpted from the foreword to the Executive Summary, by Jim Yong Kim, President, World Bank Group, prefacing the Potsdam Institute's November 2012 report to the World Bank, *Turn Down the Heat.*

> This report spells out what the world would be like if it was warmed by 4 degrees Celsius, which is what scientists are nearly unanimously predicting by the end of the century, without serious policy changes. The 4°C scenarios are devastating: the inundation of coastal cities; increasing risks for food production potentially leading to higher malnutrition rates; many dry regions becoming dryer, wet regions wetter; unprecedented heat waves in many regions, especially in the tropics; substantially exacerbated water scarcity in many regions; increased frequency of high-intensity tropical cyclones; and irreversible loss of biodiversity, including coral reef systems. And most importantly, a 4°C world is so different from the current one that it comes with high uncertainty and new risks that threaten our ability to anticipate and plan for future adaptation needs . . . Despite the global community's best intentions to keep global warming below a 2°C above pre-industrial climate, higher levels of warming are increasingly likely. Scientists agree that countries' current United Nations Framework Convention on Climate Change emission pledges and commitments would most likely result in 3.5 to 4°C warming. And the longer those pledges remain unmet, the more likely a 4°C world becomes.

The following is an excerpt from a *New Yorker* blog of November 11, 2011 by Elizabeth Kolbert, a widely published author on climate change. (http://www.newyorker.com/online/blogs/comment/2011/11two-degrees-of-disaster?)

> [In November 2011,] the Paris-based International Energy Agency released its annual *World Energy Outlook.* Among the report's key findings in that . . . global carbon-dioxide emissions rose by five per cent last year to more than thirty million metric tons . . . According to the I.E.A., "the door to two degrees Celsius

The major players in the climate change debate can be divided roughly into four groups: the scientists, the activists, the politicians, and the fossil fuel magnates. The scientists tend to be cautious and given to careful analysis. The activists are driven by a sense of urgency and the need for decisive action. The politicians are divided. Some strongly oppose any solution demanding massive government intervention and therefore refuse to acknowledge a looming catastrophe whose resolution requires it. Others emphasize the vibrancy of various forms of resistance and point to the necessity for compromise. Fossil fuel magnates, by contrast, are united in their powerful efforts to stymie any creative response whatsoever. As does the judge, these fossil fuel magnates work out of an insular self-interest. This self-interest not only submerges their ability to confront the consequences of what they are doing but also motivates them to work against the findings of climate science. (It should be evident that the present focus on fossil fuel executives has nothing to do with their personal morality and everything to do with how their current fiduciary decisions will affect the future well-being of billions of people.)

How the Illusion of Being in Control Requires Self-Deception: The Judge

Deeply puzzling is why this judge, having devoted his life to achieving a public office essential to fostering his community's cohesion, would so completely reject his heritage. Early on he was drawn to the study of the

---

is closing." The group warned that unless dramatic action is taken by 2017, so many additional billions of tons of emissions will effectively be "locked in" that a temperature increase exceeding two degrees will become inevitable . . . One of the (many) obstacles to engaging the public on the issue of climate change is that, in the context of daily life, a temperature increase of two degrees Celsius . . . sounds like no big deal . . . [However,] . . . as a group of climatologists put it on the blog *RealClimate*, "Even a 'moderate' warming of two degrees Celsius stands a strong chance of provoking drought and storm responses that could challenge civilized society, leading potentially to the conflict and suffering that go with failed states and mass migrations." . . . Rachel Warren, a researcher at the University of East Anglia, observed that "in a 4 degree Celsius world, the limits for human adaptation are likely to be exceeded in many parts of the world, while the limits for adaptation for natural systems would largely be exceeded throughout the world . . . [T]o suppose that an answer to global warming can be found by waiting is to misunderstand the nature of the problem. Once you've dumped CO_2 into the atmosphere, there's no getting it back, at least not on a human timescale. When it comes to global warming, the future really is now."

Torah and thereby to reverencing God as the source of what holds his community together. Now, by so completely rejecting God's covenant, he is undermining the very essence of what he once embraced. How does one make sense of this transformation?

One possibility is that he has become enamored of taking bribes. Such a hypothesis, however, appears too limited to account for the perverse focus of his motivation. Instead of being the lynchpin, holding together his people's concerns with the Torah's authority, he inwardly boasts of his success in breaking apart this essential connection and thereby rendering useless such an august societal resource. The entire community, not just the widow, is betrayed. Here is sabotage of the highest order.

The judge's motivations go beyond greed. His overriding purpose in life is to persuade himself that he is in control. Using his position of power, he keeps people at a distance when he wants, and compels them to come toward him when he wants. He is captivated by his illusory self-sufficiency. Perhaps his most compelling attribute is his conviction of utter independence. He will in no way submit to another's authority; no third person, no law, can possibly evoke his compliance—because he would then have to place himself under the influence of someone else.

Because he so needs to be accountable to no one, he believes he needs no one. He behaves as if he has never been an infant or a child—or will never become aged or ill. He acts as if he is independent of community, independent of the natural order, and independent of all which in that culture was perceived as provided by God. The great range of passion found, say, in the Hebrew Bible's psalmists, of despair and hope, of angst and longing, altogether elude him. These passions require the ability to rely on others; the judge's single passion is to dominate.

Because this man tries to be so completely in control, he has rendered himself completely out of control. Freed from responsibility to others, he has obliterated limits on himself. He has jettisoned every resource, all of which are derived from depending on others, to grasp the realities of his situation. He has stripped himself of every means available to him to become aware of how he alone is the creator of his imaginative world. Only by refusing everyone access, including himself, to his own doubts and uncertainties, does he succeed in maintaining his awesome illusion that he can remain above law—that is, that he can outwit reality. Where this judge sees himself as standing on a pinnacle of independence, he is instead revealed as having destroyed any place he might possibly stand. Because he is so powerful, he has also destroyed any place those reliant on him might be able to stand.

How the Illusion of Being in Control Requires Self-Deception: Fossil-Fuel Executives

One does not have to believe in a personal God to recognize that the idea of "God," in this case, of the ancient God of Israel as understood by Jesus, can be a compelling metaphor for representing the interrelatedness of all life. As the parable puts it, having "fear of God" is the same thing as having "respect for people." This combined phrasing captures the malaise of modern fossil fuel corporations. These corporations assert the rights of personhood without exercising the responsibilities of citizenship. Their leaders claim ownership of oil, gas, and coal resources it took the earth hundreds of millions of years to create. Simultaneously, these same leaders consistently evade responsibility for the consequences of releasing massive amounts of carbon into the atmosphere. Unilaterally, they have declared themselves a law unto themselves.

However, the Law these leaders dismiss is not of human origin. In the parable, the Law the judge subverts is immutable. It is the Law of God, the covenant Law that requires justice. Such reality is not established by human decision making, nor can human will alter it. It is the way things are. The consequences for ignoring it follow inexorably. To allow injustice to flourish is to foster the breakdown of human cohesiveness.[4] Similarly, the laws the fossil fuel executives ignore are equally immutable. They are the laws of physics, laws that govern how burning more and more carbon must and will raise global temperatures. Such Law, such reality, is not brought about by human decision making, nor can human will alter it. It is the way things are. The consequences for ignoring it follow inexorably.

The judge thereby becomes a fitting figure to represent the worldwide consortium of corporate fossil fuel executives who control vast sums of money with which they both expand the technology that undergirds their dominance and buy the governmental decision making that frees them to do whatever they want with that technology. No one, it seems, can overrule what they decide; almost all agree that they will have—at least in the short term—the last word.[5]

4. See Moe-Lobeda. *Resisting Structural Evil*, 41–42.

5. In the United States, leaders who head up the coal and oil industries have the

Here we come upon levels of self-deception as egregious as those found within the parable's judge. These coal and oil magnates are in no way ignorant of climate science; on the contrary, they are devoting themselves to preventing the public's awareness of that science.[6] If the science itself were unpersuasive, they would find such efforts unnecessary. At issue is no longer what the facts are but whether there exists a fundamental willingness to accept the facts.

What is the inner state of mind of these recalcitrant executives? How can they not feel—as the judge does not feel—the damage they are doing to others? Have they decided simply to turn aside from the long-term consequences of what they are doing? Rather than risk losing immediate profits, have they chosen instead to risk the future well-being of hundreds of millions of climate refugees? As with the judge, it would seem that their obligation to inquire into consequences has been replaced by a determined effort to avoid any inquiry at all.[7]

Clearly, no corporate executive could survive were he to override his fiduciary responsibility to shareholders. The corporation's primary commitment to profit making renders inconceivable any wider investment, beyond nominal charity, of its resources. Within the long history of self-interest at the foundation of modern capitalism, no mechanism has been developed able to elevate to urgent priority larger responsibility for the well-being of all humanity.

---

power to determine, through lobbying and financial contributions, crucial votes in the Senate which, under U.S. law, must ratify any climate change treaty by a two-thirds vote. Thus, through this single, singular bottleneck must first pass this nation's ability to effect climate change and, finally, to participate in determining the destiny of the entire planet for thousands of years.

6. For an in-depth documentation of how some scientists have been influenced deliberately to distort the findings of other scientists in order to cast doubt on the reality of human contributions to climate change (distortions in turn used by politicians to justify positions supporting the interests of the fossil fuel industry), see Oreskes and Conway. *Merchants of Doubt,* chapter 6. See also Coll, *Private Empire,* 77–87.

7. The Christian Right, in its own widespread denial of global warming, appears to adopt in a major way some minor added rationalizations propelling the fossil fuel magnates, namely, "I won't be here when it happens," and "I'll be able to avoid the consequences because I'll have a safe place to hide." While the oil and coal executives are merely considering both their own inevitable deaths as well as their capacity to buy protection, the Christian Right is wholly invested in the hope of life after death. Because their God will be providing them with another world, they have little motivation to save the one they already have. This kind of denial is impenetrable.

. . . . .

However, the looming crisis of climate change is now overturning this long-established relationship between profit making and self-interest. No longer is profit making simply positive and the sharing of resources simply negative. Ironically, in today's world the highest form of self-interest is altruism. If shareholders do not share, then the immediate consequences experienced by the less fortunate will eventually but inevitably be inflicted on themselves. All that is left to the fortunate is the weak margin of safety indicated by "eventually." (Twenty years? Fifty years? A hundred?) Slowly the devastation will come. In the end it will come to everyone.

Do these industry leaders actually believe that this time they alone can escape the consequences of what they are doing? Do they in fact trust their self-created illusion that they, unlike others, can evade the limits of the atmosphere's ability to absorb their poison? Are they, like the judge, so tethered to their cherished imagining of being in control that they can avoid panicked awareness of the impending catastrophe that they are themselves in the process of creating? With hundreds of millions of climate refugees on the move, do they think they will be able to maintain their positions of power? It would seem, along with the parable's judge, that many of today's fossil fuel executives believe the answer to all these questions is "Yes!" Thus the judge becomes an exceptional metaphor for the human tendency to resort to inner mendacity in a last-ditch effort to maintain the illusion of control.

The climate crisis is based on two fundamental realities. First, the concentrated accessibility of energy in the form of extremely profitable fossil fuels; and, second, the failure of human imagination to grasp the devastating consequences of burning those fuels. Substantial increases in global temperatures will lead to irreversible tipping points—that is, to physical processes that can no longer be halted or reversed. Such warming will result in the disappearance of irreplaceable glaciers—depriving 25 percent of the world's population of access to water; in the melting of polar ice—causing sea levels to rise, in turn inundating numerous major coastal cities along with massive amounts of arable land; in the melting of the tundra—releasing enormous amounts of carbon-laden methane; and in the acidification of the oceans—further curtailing the worldwide supply of food.[8] The inev-

8. Concerning these last three tipping points: 1) The polar ice that reflects heat melts into water that absorbs heat, in turn leading to the melting of even more of the remaining ice, in turn leading to increased heating of the water. "Using a conservative prediction of

itable consequence of these irreversible tipping points, subsequent to death, destruction and the massive migration of climate refugees, is the collapse of much of human civilization as we know it.

The alternatives are clear and stark.[9] Either leave 80 percent of the remaining carbon in the ground, forgo 20 trillion dollars in profits, and restore ten thousand years of relative climate sanity, or else burn that carbon, enjoy perhaps fifty years of prosperity, and then enter centuries of irreversible, multiplying catastrophes of a magnitude that will far outstrip any human capacity to adapt. This is the choice a handful of power brokers across the globe are right now having the most say in making. Because of the emerging tipping points, they have only a few years left in which to make it.

---

a half meter (20 inches) of sea-level rise, the Organization for Economic Co-operation and Development estimates that by 2070, 150 million people in the world's large port cities will be at risk from coastal flooding, along with $35 trillion worth of property—an amount that will equal 9 percent of the global GDP." (Folger, "Rising Seas," 42.) 2) The melting of the tundra will lead to release into the atmosphere of vast amounts of carbon-laden methane, in turn leading to increased melting of the tundra, and 3) the absorbing of carbon will lead to the oceans' increased acidification, in turn leading to a progressive destruction of the plankton and crustaceans at the base of the entire oceanic food chain. At some point there is no longer any way, even by vastly reducing carbon emissions, to reverse any of these processes.

9. In perhaps one of the most important articles to be published in the past decade, Bill McKibben writes:

We have five times as much oil and coal and gas on the books as climate scientists think is safe to burn. We'd have to keep 80 percent of those reserves locked away underground to avoid that fate. Before we knew those numbers, our fate had been likely. Now, barring some massive intervention, it seems certain . . . Given this hard math, we need to view the fossil-fuel industry in a new light. It has become a rogue industry, reckless like no other force on Earth. It is Public Enemy Number One to the survival of our planetary civilization . . . They're clearly cognizant of global warming . . . And yet they relentlessly search for more hydrocarbons. In early March, [2012,] Exxon CEO Rex Tillerson told Wall Street analysts that the company plans to spend $37 billion a year through 2016 (about $100 million a day) searching for yet more oil and gas. There's not a more reckless man on the planet than Tillerson. Late last month . . . he told a New York audience that global warming is real, but dismissed it as an "engineering problem" that has "engineering solutions." Such as? "Changes to weather patterns that move crop-production areas around—we'll adapt to that," Tillerson said . . . "The fear factor that people want to throw out there to say, 'We just have to stop this,' I do not accept." Of course not—if he did accept it, he'd have to keep his reserves in the ground. (McKibben, "Global Warming's," 58–59)

To quote a blogger named David Roberts, "We are stuck between temperatures we can't possibly accommodate and carbon reduction pathways we can't possibly achieve."

Here is but one example of how modern fossil fuel leaders are relentlessly pursuing their efforts to extract and burn intolerable amounts of carbon. In the early 2000s, Lee Raymond was the chief executive officer of ExxonMobil, the largest and most powerful of the big oil corporations. Nicknamed "Iron Ass" by his subordinates, Raymond was well known both for disagreeing with the science of global warming and for disseminating doubt about climate change. At the same time, in an effort to get the jump on competitors, he was overseeing a team of researchers using that same science to predict how climate change "might alter surface and ocean trends and lead the corporation to new oil fields."[10] Raymond's arrogance, like that of the judge, is breathtaking. Instead of recognizing in the scientific research an urgent warning to slow the drilling for oil, he co-opts this same research to increase the drilling for oil. He will bend the laws of physics to submit to his will.

The judge's elevation of his own creature comfort over the cohesion of his community stands as a powerful metaphor for the choice many fossil fuel executives are now making. His way of being represents how a small minority can elevate immediate perspectives above the well-being of the world's people, both living and unborn. The only difference between the judge and fossil fuel executives is found the degree of havoc each can wreak.

Not only is the judge a metaphor for blatant disregard of God's Law, he is an astonishingly accurate image of one who, at the same time as he destroys, is in fact honored. Within the stringent brevity of the parable, hidden between the powerful judge and the deprived widow is a whole array of persons actively supporting the judge's dominance. The judge succeeds in maintaining his arrogance because large swathes of the privileged of his era agree with his way of being. Similarly, because contemporary society wants the fossil fuel executives to mine all the carbon under their control (thereby bringing about worldwide havoc and death), they are not viewed as dangerous. On the contrary, they are regarded, at least by the elite, as respected citizens.

In Jesus's time there was a sharp divide between a minute aristocracy and a great mass of impoverished peasants, artisans, and slaves. The modern situation in the United States is different, with the presence of a large middle class, wealthy by any global standard, who are immersed in a culture of out-of-control consumerism, involving, among other things, a myriad of fossil fuel products from plastics and fertilizers to gasoline to the

10. Cited in Coll, *Private Empire*, 185–86.

diesel fuel that propels the trucks that supply the shopping malls. Lodged securely inside the center of this culture, the fossil fuel executives are supported by the widely accepted ideology of modern capitalism. At the heart of that ideology is the idea that economies should keep on growing—and for that they must have vast new amounts of energy.

The irony here is riveting. By wanting more, namely, more energy by burning more carbon, we will assuredly receive less, namely, a degraded planet unable to support human civilization as we know it. In an era when multiplying population and increased demand has for some time outstripped the Earth's capacities to provide, emphasis on growth is only now being recognized as a major source of our headlong rush to self-destruction. Because our planet can no longer support such continued growth, this wanting of more has become the amoral, structural evil of our time. In this way the judge's shortsighted quest for skin-comfort becomes an exceptional image for our insistent focus on immediate gratification at the cost of eventual self-destruction.

Among his surviving narrative parables, this one is among Jesus's shortest—and most important. Within the space of a few sentences, he has evoked enormously problematic worlds—his and ours—where lawlessness has so overtaken Law that fantasy has trumped reality. Unlike in his other parables, here Jesus is no longer with irony satirizing a corrupt vineyard owner or an imperialist talent master, figures who inhabit the more accessible domains of lawbreaking. With the character of the judge, he has advanced to describe someone far more dangerous. Here he has created a powerful figure of central influence who altogether disregards Law, that is, someone who wantonly dismisses the realities of what human community and human cohesion require. For the first time in these stories, Jesus steps out of the shadows of irony and instead shines a direct light on the human capacity for inner deception.

The Widow

After evoking the enormous power of the judge, Jesus delineates the sharply limited options available to the widow. Whether she is seeking vengeance or justice, her quest enters a world in which any appeal to God's law is massively denied. Her powerlessness is defined not so much by her economic or social position as it is by the judge's breathtaking evacuation of law.

Under normal circumstances, such a completely powerless person would either be silenced by despair or compelled to retreat. In the character of the widow, Jesus introduces someone whose power lies in not being cowed. Those in control, like the judge, have systematically insulated themselves from such persons. In response, the widow will insist on being seen.[11] She digs in and fights. Her severely constricted action, like David's small stone in the narrowly exposed forehead of the armored Goliath, seems to break through miraculously. But where David felled his opponent with a single blow, the widow is reduced to becoming an effete battering ram. The Greek verb *hupōpiadzō*, translated here as "wearing out" ("I will grant her justice, so that she may not wear me out by continually coming") literally means "to strike under the eye."

The image comes from prizefighting. The verb places the widow in a boxing ring, jabbing repeatedly at the eye socket of the judge. She is determined; she is tenacious. Unlike Goliath, however, the judge does not fall; at any moment he could as easily crush her as vindicate her. She wins, not as a consequence of the judge's respect for law, nor through political influence, nor through bribery, but simply because she has been able, at great risk to herself, to make this powerful man feel uncomfortable. What should have been the straightforward product of a well-established order has collapsed into the accidental consequence of one individual's lonely persistence.

What exactly is the widow trying to elicit? The Greek verb *ekdikeō*, indicating what the widow is after, is ambiguous. *Ek* means "out of" or "away from" and *dikaios* means "right" or "obligatory in view of certain requirements of justice." Allied with the verbs incorporating *dikeō* that were examined in chapter 4, *ekdikeō* can mean either "to avenge someone" or "to procure justice for someone." Given this ambiguity, what is driving the widow's persistence can be understood in at least two distinct ways: (1) she is seeking revenge, that is, for the judge to punish someone who has harmed her, or (2) she is seeking justice, that is, for the judge to recover for her what someone has taken from her. Among persons everywhere who go to court, feelings can range from hurt at not being recognized to anger at being deprived to rage at being damaged.[12] Mitigation requires, at the very least, access to law. Systematic blockage from law can convert feelings of hurt into demands for vengeance.

11. For portions of this paragraph I am indebted to Karen L. Ford.
12. See the parallel range of responses to persecution outlined in the appendix.

It is unclear whether the widow's focus is on arousing violence or restoring fairness. How one chooses to account for the widow's motivation matters. If she is attempting to persuade the judge to impose a gratifying retaliation, she is entering a circular world with no exit. She, the oppressed, is on the way to becoming an oppressor.

What if, instead, the widow is seeking some rebalance of the way things should be between the powerful and the powerless? This second understanding introduces a richer set of possibilities. Here, she is attempting the creative work that beckons every person ever subjected to lawlessness. Here, her quest for a more present equity embraces the potential to ward off future violence. Here, in terms of this chapter's theme, her resolute but exhausting action represents every modern initiative reaching out to effect climate justice. Her persistence is a thin thread of hope connected to the potential hawser of aroused public opinion that might finally drag the judge off his pedestal of imperturbable self-sufficiency. Now, as then, those who are battered in their attempts to challenge lawlessness need the sustained infusion of determination and courage.

However, at least two major differences exist between ancient conditions and modern reality. The first is that the widow, along with the Third World, the poor, and minorities, have as a resource their anger. By contrast, members of the American middle class are called upon to give up some of what they already have. That such a letting go leads to possessing more is at the heart of Jesus's whole way of being. For him such a strategy is founded on the trustworthiness of God. The second major difference between then and now is how developing such an awareness—how releasing one's grip can result in having more—requires time, great amounts of time. In this era of rapidly advancing, irreversible tipping points, almost no time remains.[13]

---

13. Readers may compare how the two types of contemporary government possessing the greatest concentrations of global power are positioned to respond when confronting this devastatingly urgent challenge. On the one hand, Western democracies, far more advanced in their respect for human rights, have in major ways been outmaneuvered by the crafted denial of global corporations, which corporations, in turn, exercise their power by subverting vulnerable democratic institutions. On the other hand, Chinese Communist leaders, notorious for denying human rights, control a centralized, monolithic power base. Already perceiving in the warnings of climate science serious threats to their own self-interest, they are positioned to counter, without obligation to shareholders, the power of Chinese corporate self-interest. They are also able to impose top-down, authoritarian interventions, in turn requiring major sacrifices, which a vast population, left to their own preferences, would certainly resist.

At some point in our future, three or four generations from now, the vindictive and restorative possibilities found among the widow's options will merge at an exponentially increasing pace. As millions of climate refugees flood into established communities, deprivation and violence will so overwhelm fairness and equity that another tipping point will have been reached. At that point we will abandon further attempts to unite around the shared acceptance of limit and instead fragment into competing groups to fight for receding control over diminishing resources.

The Seeming Inability to Prevent Tragedy: The Parable

When the parable ends, nothing in fact has changed. Although she has secured vindication, the widow's success is based not on inviolable law but on the rotting foundation of one individual's creature comfort. That the judge vindicates her is a sop. Why he does so remains the fundamental issue. His allegiance to what is lawful is paper thin; it will disappear as soon as the pressure recedes—because this supposed authority will acknowledge obligation to no one other than himself. By rendering his decision based merely on self-interest, he continues to obliterate his people's access to law. At the parable's close the judge, without hope of change, is still encased in entitlement—and the surrounding community, without hope of change, is still deprived of justice.

The Seeming Inability to Prevent Tragedy: Fossil-Fuel Executives—along with the Rest of Us

At the same time that more and more people are agreeing that humans are responsible for climate change,[14] opportunities effectively to intervene are becoming increasingly limited. Time is of the essence. A handful of power brokers across the globe have less than a handful of years in which to avert irreversible outcomes. As one writer puts it, "We are on the hinge of history."

While dismissing the laws of physics will inevitably result in reality's lashing back, reality will begin that lashing on the backs of the poor. Only later will consequences intrude upon the rich. However, by the time the rich nations recognize their peril, it will be too late, because the cascading

14. See, for example, Miller. "Weather Gone Wild."

crises of multiple, irreversible tipping points will overrun the capacities of every nation on earth to adapt.[15] By the time we finally become certain, by the time we at long last join together in an imperative determination to make major sacrifices, we will have by our delay rendered ourselves impotent to produce any decisive change.

Epilogue

The figure of the corrupt judge has been with us from the beginning of civilization; throughout the ages he has kept intact his illusion of control. Endlessly able to break God's Law of human interdependence, he appears even now to be succeeding in defeating God's desire. He still believes that he can divide humanity into those many on the outside who are bereft and those few on the inside who hoard privilege. However, with the advent of global warming, for the first time in human history, everyone is trapped in the same space. The boundaries between inside and outside no longer hold. Unlike all previous encounters between human entitlement and God's longing, this time no one will escape the consequences. If we do not act as one, soon, and with great sacrifice, gradually but inexorably the now silenced widow Earth will roar back upon us all, full throated and open throttled. Then no one, either outside or inside, will be able to stand.

It is a stunning vision that Jesus offers: this rogue judge trying to render useless the centuries-old, magnificent, all-embracing, revered Torah—just as today a miniscule group of oil and coal barons are trying to render useless the centuries-old, magnificent, all-embracing, revered scientific method. Shockingly, within the confines of the parable, as this powerful man proceeds to impose his all-encompassing rejection of God's Law, God does not intervene. While this idea may be of little import to nonreligious people who have never considered any other possibility, it profoundly challenges long-standing Christian expectations that God will act unilaterally to make things right—either here or hereafter.

Unlike the story of the widow in 1 Kings, where God rescues the widow, Jesus here portrays no hint of God's intervention; he stringently blocks any introduction of a divine power that rescues. Luke cannot abide this possibility. As an underwater swimmer breaks to the surface gasping for air, so Luke strains to infuse a divine intervention to relieve the suffocating

15. Here see Oreskes and Conway, *Collapse of Western Civilization.*

exclusion locked inside this narrative.[16] In his commentary immediately following the parable (Luke 18:6–8), penned perhaps eighty years after Jesus told this story, Luke simply replaces the lawlessness of the unrighteous judge with the deliverance of a deeply concerned deity.

· · · · ·

However, in his attempt to rescue the parable, Luke has violated a carefully fabricated limit. Nowhere in the story itself is there any hint of provision from the outside; nothing in it suggests access to another world, a different regime, a new law.[17] From the beginning to the end of this strikingly provocative narrative, Jesus insists on enclosing his listeners in a painful dilemma. Whoever enters its space is overtaken by an urgent desire to break down its walls, to bring in some outsider who will overcome its corruption and establish justice. That Jesus so stringently blocks such outside intervention is unusually compelling.

The way Jesus's parables work portrays his understanding of how God works. His parables never coerce; instead they evoke, they stir, they arouse. In Jesus's vision, evidenced by Jesus's whole way of being, God is found outside the corridors of power so completely occupied by the judge and the fossil fuel barons. In Jesus's vision, as Luke confirms, God is instead found alongside the poor, the dispossessed, and the oppressed. Although God will not intervene, God is assuredly with the widow. Whether this powerless person is violent in response to violence or destitute in response to deprivation, God endures her ordeal, aghast at the paucity of what she receives. Because she experiences no restoration of covenant practice, no restitution

16. Appended to this parable, in Luke 18:6–8, is commentary purportedly spoken by Jesus. However, Jesus rarely, if ever, seeks to resolve the difficulties his parables create. I follow those who believe these verses are part of a later tradition. See, for example, Funk et al, eds, *Parables*, 41, 106. Drury, *Parables*, 153, suggests that "a very probable source" for this commentary is Sirach 35:15–19: "for the Lord is the judge, and with him is no partiality . . . He will not ignore the supplication of . . . the widow when she pours out her complaint."

17. The story of the Friend at Midnight (Luke 11:5–8), seemingly similar to the present parable, is also used by Luke to exemplify the theme of persistence in prayer. In it a recalcitrant neighbor late at night is finally persuaded to unbolt his door and give bread to a shamelessly importuning householder so that the latter can provide hospitality to an unexpected guest. The striking contrast here concerns the presence or absence of the community's "law," i.e., of the codes operative in peasant life of honor/shame and hospitality, which the neighbor, altogether unlike the judge, respects.

of God's Law, but only a paltry vindication based solely on one individual's self-centered comfort, God sits down beside the widow and weeps.

Could this parable be reflecting Jesus's understanding of how his God will not wrest open our shortsightedness, overcome our self-centeredness, and coerce our responsiveness; of how his God, while steadfastly holding out to us possibilities for what we can and must do, will not compel us to embrace these possibilities? When limiting God's intervention, Jesus in no way limits God's presence in our lives or God's longing for the well-being of all creation. By allowing us to destroy God's covenant, by permitting us to disdain God's kingdom, by yielding to our devastating overriding of God's Law, God, of course, is not defeated. Rather, we are found to be defeating ourselves in God's grieving presence. Bereft of irony, listeners are here lured, finally, to imagine the awesome extent of divine distress.

11

Summaries of This Book's Interpretations

BEGINNING AT LEAST AS far back as Mark's Gospel, the work of understanding Jesus's parables has involved a further shaping of what has been only partially shaped. Interpreters must transform ambiguity into evocativeness disciplined by coherence. Readers realize that they too must weigh options and choose among them. We are thereby positioned to observe the ways we listen. By becoming more aware of how we listen, we enhance the ways we grasp the world around us.

These two goals—providing challenging parable interpretations and expanding readers ways of listening—are at the center of this book. They converge to provide one answer to the question, Where in these narratives is their power to effect change? Spelled out in detail in chapter 12, the short answer is, by entering more deeply into the work of listening, listeners change.

The previous chapters have probed each story and tested each result in relation to a major global issue. These last two chapters move beyond the particularities of any given parable in an effort to discover, both in their content and in the work they pose for listeners, their shared structures. In preparation for such a quest, below are offered summaries of this book's interpretations. For readers to have a better chance of discerning how these separate understandings may resonate with each other, they are here placed side by side. At the expense of repetition, such juxtaposing offers a more concise basis on which to evaluate how much the putative shared structures described in chapter 12 have been imposed by the author and how much they are essential to the stories themselves.

Chapter 1: Tenants and a Landlord, Iraq and the United States (The Wicked Tenants)

Comprehending this parable's tragedy calls for grappling with the lengthy sequence lodged within its narrow boundaries. Parable listeners are called upon to reach beyond the immediate murder to ponder a long history of domination. However, just as the parable's landlord and just as our leaders who invaded Iraq ignored the prior histories of their own violence, so listeners are similarly tempted to disregard such violence. Then a small group of aristocrats chronically stole the land of peasant smallholders; now the West has engaged in persistent efforts over decades to wrest control of Iraqi oil. Instead, listeners are drawn to focus simply on the violent response of the victim (then, the tenants' unexpected murdering; now, the unanticipated strife following Saddam Hussein's overthrow).

To grasp the parable's power is to grasp its irony. Because he so much wants to believe his imperialism is within the scope of law, a landlord exposes his son to lethal lawlessness. By persuading themselves they are providing democracy while remaining passively participant in an unjust reach for control of Iraqi oil, the American people join this father in belatedly discovering they have in fact been the perpetrators of their own loss.

Chapter 2: Slaves and a Master, the Sudan and China (The Talents)

In this metaphor, tax revenues are first sucked up by the slave master (Roman overlords), with some of the profits being remaindered to necessary intermediaries (Jewish aristocrats). Similarly, Sudanese oil is first sucked up by the Chinese government, with some of the profits being remaindered to necessary intermediaries (the genocidal government in Khartoum).

The third slave's response to his master's imperialism is at the center of the parable's ambiguity. Limited by his vulnerability to the single option of passive resistance, he mounts a carefully disguised attack upon his lord's presumption. He will not, as do his exploiting fellows, exploit. He will refuse to impose on others what has been perpetrated upon himself. In response, the dominating slave master is incensed that one of his dominated slaves does not follow his example. Listeners are drawn to side with the slave master, who in turn rejects, just as much now as then, a courageous whistle-blower who in fact risks everything in a superbly crafted, seemingly ineffective effort to resist his superior's oppression.

Jesus thus envelops his listeners in pressures similar to those the master imposes on his slave—that is, similar to those empire inflicts on everyone who is instrumental in serving its greed. Exploit, keep distance from your inherent criminality, and you will be rewarded. Resist, stand up for the exploited, and you will either be ignored or hammered into the ground.

Steven Spielberg's challenge to Chinese enabling of Sudanese genocide seems as quixotic as this slave's crafted challenge to Jewish collusion with Roman oppression. Both men nonviolently confront overpowering violence. Both do so with the same seeming ineffectiveness as did the author of the parable himself when, in the final days before his death, he overturned the tables inside the courtyard of the Jerusalem temple.

Chapter 3: Jesus's Parable of the Talents; the Imaging and Mimicry of Empire

At empire's narrow apex are found the exploiting slave master and his well-appointed slaves—that is, the Roman overlords and their aristocratic Jewish clients. At its base is the inarticulate mass of peasants required to create the expropriated wealth.

The slave master's description of his behavior stands as an unchallenged expression of imperialism's entitlement. "I reap," he says, "where I did not sow." Central to this parable's functioning, and to the functioning of empire everywhere, is the absence of any law capable of challenging this aristocrat's lawless abuse.

Hiding behind a facade of inaction, the third slave resists his master's demand to exploit. To see him as a coward is to be co-opted by the insidious power of imperial domination. If listeners are to penetrate the seeming incompetence masking his courageous risk taking, they must first break through similar distortions imposed on the slave by empire's prior coercion.

This imaging and mimicking of empire by Jesus is magnificent, his indirectness breathtaking, and his relevance for today stunning.

Chapter 4: Laborers and a Vineyard Owner, Iraqi Oil and the United States (The Vineyard Workers)

A vineyard owner sincerely believes his momentary generosity will overcome his chronic depriving. His long-standing wage of a denarius a day will barely sustain life. The owner creates his false drama in order to justify his ongoing resistance to paying a living wage. At the expense of imposing shame on those he controls, he attempts to persuade the world around him that he is a good person.

Deceived by his self-convinced and convincing drama, listeners back off any nascent challenge to the owner's unjust aggrandizing. Instead they are lured into applauding a demeaning generosity designed to cover up a compromised honor. In similar fashion the American public is co-opted by their government's hollow claims to be exporting democracy into surrendering protest when confronting its efforts to steal Iraqi oil. *What* is going on can be described simply: "You are stealing our labor." "You are stealing our oil." Becoming able *to see* what is going on is much, much more difficult. Listeners are called upon to challenge what in fact are skillfully constructed, effectively imposed cover-ups.

Chapter 5: A Woman with Leaven, a Woman with a Jar, and a Man with a Sword; Gender Inequities

The parable of the Leaven evokes the joy of a woman's pregnancy. The parable of the Jar evokes the tragedy of a woman's miscarriage. The parable of the Sword evokes the conflicts inherent in male dominance.

The Leaven describes how human initiative can intertwine with nature in acts of creativity that are available to anyone willing to contribute within the limits of the created order.

The Jar encloses both loss and shame. It describes the double desolation of every person experiencing catastrophe. Thus the Jar may be seen as standing between the Leaven and the Sword and questioning both. Does God indeed not intervene when the creation, under human stewardship, so badly miscarries? Does God stand aside while our heritage spills out on the ground? Or does God instead sit down beside the woman with her broken jar—and weep?

When we consider God's reliance on human initiative, we are tempted to rush to the side of assertiveness. In response, the Sword asks, can justice be established through courageous violence without falling prey to corrupting coercion? If we destroy (rather than transform) the powerful other, we render ourselves vulnerable both to further destroying and to being destroyed.

These three shorter parables function as sounding boards for some of the longer parables in this book.

When the woman buries her yeast in dough, her action results in a gratifying fecundity. When the slave buries his talent in the ground, he brings forth nothing at all. Yet, in his corrupted world, to invest is to exploit while to abort is to heal.

The woman's broken jar, her betrayed trust in the integrity of her body, alludes to the breakdown in trust between a father and his son. What the son should have retained—his inheritance—leaks shamefully through his fingers. Should the woman have examined her jar more carefully? Or has the jar failed the woman? Has the son betrayed his father? Or has the father failed to be with his son in the midst of the son's as yet incomplete becoming?

In the parable of the Sword, the courageous man who dares to destroy the strong man's body evokes the tenants who dare to destroy their landlord's son. But is not attack precisely what power provokes? The twin forms of violence, that from below and that from above, are now poised to reverberate endlessly.

The woman with the jar, who has done nothing wrong, is left immersed in shame, whereas the man with the sword, a murderer, walks away erect with pride. When these parables are placed side by side, with what provocativeness do they reflect the gender inequities of the ancient, and modern, world!

Chapter 6: A Slave and a Master, Main Street and Wall Street (The Unforgiving Slave)

One is bewildered by the foolhardiness of this parable's competent slave. His master has just released him from an enormous debt. Should he not then, out of gratitude, have imitated his master? Instead, he stupidly cashiers a colleague in easy view of his recently magnanimous lord. Impressed by the master's generosity, listeners readily agree with this overlord that he should have been able, through one truly exceptional gesture, to alter his slave's life-long pattern of imitating his master's domination.

Following the Wall Street crisis of September 2008, Congress approved a $700 billion taxpayer bailout. In the months that followed, when unemployment rose, home foreclosures grew, and businesses could not borrow, the nation's top bankers paid themselves over $2 billion in bonuses.

Public outrage was intense. Yet any close observer of Wall Street would re-tort, "Yes, it was a hugely generous rescue. But what in the world did you imagine these multimillionaire barons would do—except keep on taking more and more for themselves?" Main Street's extraordinary releasing of an immense debt turned out to be altogether impotent to transform Wall Street's embedded culture of greed.

When the slave master releases his slave's debt, listeners in fact confront a truly remarkable choice. For at this moment they must decide whether this lord's singular act of generosity indeed has the power to wrest apart ancient slavery's iron law of ruthlessness. Does not the master's releasing so enfold his own continuing assumption of dominance that its effectiveness is vitiated? By focusing attention on the slave's ungrateful response, listen-ers are diverted from perceiving how the master's inability to relinquish his own life of coercion renders him impotent to release the same in his slave.

When we turn back, finally, to the slave, all that is left is the massive irony of a masterful slave being tortured by his imperious slave master for having imitated his master.

Chapter 7: A Manager and a Rich Man, Afghanistan and the United States (The Dishonest Steward)

A rich man, full of neglect towards his competent subordinate, cashiers him for neglect. It is left to listeners to discern how the manager's squandering of property comes in response to the rich man's squandering of concern. Jesus hides evidence of the rich man's neglect inside three clues: (1) The rich man, on his own, does not know that his manager is wasting his goods. (2) Once informed, he reacts immediately as if the charges were true. (3) He demonstrates no awareness of how his formerly trusted manager might feel upon being dismissed; he thereby fails to protect himself from the lat-ter's betrayal.

A contemporary example of such a long and complex sequence of trust, abandonment, collapse, and blame may be found in the experience of Hamid Karzai, effectively appointed president of Afghanistan by the United States. Refusing to provide him with the economic resources essential to any success, the United States has demanded of him results that are impos-sible to achieve. As does the manager's squandering, so Karzai's wasting of opportunity indicates neither malevolence nor incompetence but rather a remarkable flailing.

Jesus distracts his listeners one last time with the rich man's unexpected praise. Ironically, the rich man also hopes that his commendation will divert those around him from noticing how all along his growing neglect has been at the center of his manager's collapse. In the end the manager is destroyed while the rich man departs, as does the United States, defrauded and aggrieved. As in the parable so in the present, the one dominating reduces the one dominated to incompetence—all the while declaring the unfortunate subordinate to be the one responsible.

Listeners must labor at length to achieve coherence in a tragedy so difficult to comprehend. They are called upon to probe the inner workings of the parable with a sustained attention that is completely lacking inside the parable itself. The skill of the narrator is extraordinary.

Chapter 8: A Younger Son and a Father (The Prodigal Son)

A loving father gives to his son his *bios*, his life. To be chosen this way, by capitulation from above to an impetuous demand from below, can have unexpectedly devastating consequences. For the son to be provided with what is not yet his to possess is for him to be confronted with a double-barreled paternal judgment: (1) his father has lost confidence in his own becoming, and (2) his father expects his son can produce nothing of worth on his own. The father fails to suspect that his undisciplined generosity towards his undisciplined son may in fact destroy any chance the son has to develop some discipline of his own.

Jesus entrusts to his listeners the work of pondering the responsibilities of *both* father and son. Certainly the son has the obligation to engage the consequences of his own immaturity; however, equally certain is how the father also has the obligation to confront his damaging need to be needed. The father has imposed a largess pivotal to his son's ensuing collapse. In the midst of celebrating, the father continues to be unaware of his role in humiliating. Bereft of a father who understands, the son must struggle alone with his shame.

This interpretation builds on a supposition supported by this book's understanding of all its other parables, namely, that Jesus in this beloved story is being ironic. He has created a narrative in which there is more than meets the eye. He is interrogating established understandings of the Genesis accounts of a father and two sons—stories of how God gives the inheritance (that is, the Land) to the younger son (that is, to his chosen people).

In so doing Jesus is engaging perhaps the central question of the Torah, namely, how does the God of some become the God of all? In this reading, the parable is portraying not how God in fact gives and forgives but rather how God is prevented from giving and forgiving because the parable's listeners have learned to believe in a god who divides the inheritance, that is, in a god who prefers some over others. What if we dare perceive our god as choosing us over others? What dangers face any nation imagining itself divinely privileged? Jesus's parable proffers the inevitable consequences, namely, a faulty giving, a failed receiving, and an impotent forgiving. This same challenge, which Jesus may here be posing to his own tradition, is one addressed with equal potency to a Western Christendom that has inherited, prematurely, dominion over the earth.

Chapter 9: The Poor and a Householder, the Third World and Debt (The Great Banquet)

Because he so much wants to control through his generosity the lost recognition he seeks, a householder fails to evaluate the impact of his participation in fostering the impoverishment of the very poor he has so magnificently welcomed. He seeks to enliven in the destitute respect towards himself by relying on resources that the poor will eventually suspect he has long ago stolen from them. His effort to repossess his honor will inevitably come into conflict with the suppressed resentment of those to whom he gives. His quest for respect will founder on his taking for granted his innocence.

Similarly, any generosity to the Third World from the First is undermined by First World's taking far more in debt service than it gives in aid. Through the impersonal workings of First World financial structures, millions of poor people in the Third World, for their own lifetimes and the lifetimes of their children, have become required to pay to the rich of the industrialized world endless amounts of interest on debts for which they are in no way responsible.

In the parable's terms, can the householder overcome with his charity the long-standing inequities embedded in his economic dominance? In contemporary terms, can we in the First World win respect through our aid without first honoring the consequences of our own prior imperialism?

Chapter 10: A Widow and a Judge, Climate Change and Fossil Fuel Executives (The Unjust Judge)

A seemingly self-sufficient judge demeans a reliance on community that in fact constitutes the very foundation of his independence. The judge presumes that he is obligated to no tradition whatsoever. He understands himself as self-originating. By trying to be in complete control, he has become completely out of control. He provides an exceptional metaphor for the human tendency to resort to inner mendacity in an effort to maintain the illusion of control. Only by refusing everyone access (including himself) to his own doubts and uncertainties does he succeed in maintaining the awesome illusion that he can stand above law—and thereby outwit reality.

Just as the judge disdains the laws of God, so in our time, concerning climate change, fossil fuel executives disdain the laws of physics. It is a stunning vision: a rogue judge trying to render useless the centuries-old, magnificent, and revered Torah—just as today a handful of oil and coal magnates are trying to render useless the centuries-old, magnificent, and revered scientific method. Whether the widow is seeking vengeance or justice, her quest must be undertaken in a world in which any appeal to God's law is massively undermined. Similar ponderous denial now confronts all who seek to represent the inexorable laws of physics. How has this judge, and we along with him, reached such a place of destroying that which so crucially nourishes us?

This parable reflects Jesus's understanding of how his God will not break through human shortsightedness or coerce human responsiveness. Within the confines of the parable, as this powerful man proceeds to impose his all-encompassing rejection of God's law, God does not intervene.

Nonetheless, God is assuredly *with* the widow and *with* the surrounding community deprived of law. By allowing us to destroy God's covenant, by yielding to our selfish and devastating efforts to overpower natural law, God, of course, is not defeated. Rather, we shall defeat ourselves in God's grieving presence. Sitting beside the widow, God raises her eyes—and looks to us to intervene.

12

The Luring of Jesus and the Longing of God

RAISING HIS HAND IN class, a college sophomore asked, "If Jesus knew what the kingdom of God was, why didn't he just say so?" Engaging far more complexity than this student could possibly have imagined, his question challenges anyone seeking to answer it. For here is being wondered not only *what,* in Jesus's understanding, is coming in "the kingdom of God," or *how* it is coming, or *where* is it coming, or *when* is it coming, but also *why* Jesus does not provide these wanted descriptions more directly.

Pondering the past fifty years of literature debating what Jesus meant by "the kingdom of God," Bruce Chilton has remarked, "In that literature, as within the scholarly discussion it reflects, what is striking is the absorption of attention by the issue of *when* the kingdom is conceived of as coming in Jesus' understanding."[1]

Jesus's conception of the kingdom of God was at the heart of his teaching. A more adequate understanding of what he intended might be discovered by placing less emphasis on wondering *When* does God's reign come? (using questions such as, Has it already come? or Is it coming now? or Will it come in the future?) Instead more emphasis might be placed on wondering *How* does God's reign come? (thereby developing questions such as, Does it come through God's imposing? or Does it come through God's yearning?) Subsequent wondering about *What* is it that is coming? then yields questions such as, Did Jesus anticipate a suddenly perfect society? or Was he describing multiple processes of healing and reconciliation leading to ongoing increments in sharing and equality?

1. Chilton, "Kingdom of God," 256.

Embedded in the above interrogation is a further question: does God's domain come to us, or do we enter God's domain? Here the concept of coming is placed in tension with the concept of entering. These seeming polarities may be understood as complementary. We cannot enter God's domain unless God comes to us. God cannot come to us unless we enter God's domain. This concluding chapter embraces a parallel approach for understanding these parables. We cannot enter them unless they come to us as they are—that is, as incomplete and beckoning. They cannot come to us in their fullness unless we welcome that incompleteness and engage that beckoning.

How the Kingdom of God Comes and How the Parables Come

A dominant consensus among New Testament scholars across a major portion of the twentieth century was that the historical Jesus expected the end of history as we know it to be both imminent and brought about by the unilateral, overpowering intervention of God. Then, beginning slowly in midcentury and gaining momentum by its end came the development of a different consensus, namely, that the historical Jesus was focused on the immediate, here-and-now advent of the reign of God, a coming that was available to all who were open to reach for it.[2]

Playing a major role in this shifting consensus was a revised way of understanding Jesus's parables, which earlier had been read as allegories for a future judgment. One important pioneer in this revision was Amos N. Wilder, who was a leader in the Parables Seminar of the Society of Biblical Literature in the 1960s and 1970s.

> Wilder argued that the parables are narrative metaphors—that is, stories through which the world of God's kingdom might come to life in the imagination of the listener. This idea, now widely accepted, was related to the . . . idea that Jesus spoke not of a future, apocalyptic event, but of the immediate reign of God, now present

---

2. For an excellent overview of the history of this scholarly debate, see the editor's introduction in Miller, ed. *Apocalyptic Jesus*, 1–13. For a groundbreaking essay developing this new consensus, see Borg, "Temperate Case." An exhaustive review of the textual sources underlying the debate may be found in Crossan, *Historical Jesus*, chapter 11, "John and Jesus" and chapter 12, "Kingdom and Wisdom." For another valuable overview of these same issues, see Patterson, *God of Jesus*, chapter 5, "On Jesus and the End of the World."

in the potential of the human imagination to see the world differently and to act accordingly.[3]

Located inside the larger question of whether the historical Jesus
imagined God's reign as coming through divine imposition or, by contrast,
through a noncoercive inviting is the question of how he imagined the recipient's response to come about. This book proposes that for Jesus, the
"how" of the way God invites us to enter his domain is intimately related to
the "how" of the way Jesus invites us to enter his parables.

How God's rule comes toward us is essentially reflected in how we are
expected to embrace it. The two general options are by being compelled
to (for example, by the advent of overwhelming beauty) or by seeking to.
Similarly, how Jesus's parables come toward us is essentially reflected in
how we are expected to embrace them. The two general options are by being confronted with unavoidable meaning or by having to work to discover
possible meaning.

Thus, when engaging Jesus's parables, we can notice how our own responses come about. Are we required to see things in a certain way, or are
we free to choose? Following our initial puzzlement, how much work are
we willing to do before we choose? (Put another way, what is the nature of
our contribution?) We can then realize that (1) we do not have to interpret
any given parable in any particular way, and (2) we must still make choices.
We can then become aware both of the choices we make and of the degree
of energy we put into making them.

Two Ways of Understanding Jesus's Parables

The debate that ranged across the twentieth century and is outlined above
resonates with two very different ways we can go about understanding the
parables studied in this book. By far the most popular is to see them as
metaphors representing the utterly unexpected and altogether gracious interventions of a loving God. This understanding discovers a God who sacrifices the life of his beloved son (the Wicked Tenants), a God who rewards
those who are faithful (the Talents), a God who is generous to those who
are last (the Vineyard Workers), a God who releases an astounding debt
(the Unforgiving Slave), a God who commends those who are prudent (the
Dishonest Steward), a God who forgives the wayward (the Prodigal Son),

---

3. Stephen J. Patterson, quoted in Miller, *Apocalyptic Jesus*, 71.

a God who provides extraordinary largess (the Great Banquet), and a God who answers persistent prayer (the Unjust Judge). Hearing the parables in these ways, listeners experience first of all God's compassionate intervening.

By contrast, it is equally possible to find in these parables the precise opposite of such divine provision. They may instead be understood as describing the varied ways humans dismiss God's desire in order to dominate one another: how the powerful suck up law for themselves and leave others lawless (the Wicked Tenants); how the powerful suck up wealth for themselves and leave others impoverished (the Talents); how the powerful suck up repute for themselves and leave others shamed (the Vineyard Workers, the Unforgiving Slave, the Dishonest Steward, and—just possibly—the Prodigal Son and the Great Banquet), and how the powerful suck up control for themselves and leave others bereft (the Unjust Judge). Hearing the parables in these ways, listeners experience first of all the endless corruption in human hierarchies.

The Work of Parable Listeners: Part 1

Centering on the maldistribution of wealth, Jesus's parables offer revolutionary potential hidden within ironic indirection. Here the pathway is anything but straightforward. Jesus frames each of these narratives by placing two characters, an overlord and an underling, in situations where, across large differences in wealth and power, each must rely on the other. Allowing no one from the outside to intervene, Jesus encases these two figures in closed worlds of unrelieved tragedy.

Replicating the strategy of imperial elites in every era, Jesus permits only the corrupt superior to define what is going on. Far from challenging the elite's spurious descriptions, Jesus instead gives these distortions pride of place. By leaving the characterizing of what is happening entirely in the hands of the dominant character, Jesus entices his listeners to imagine that these superior figures are in fact capable of making things right. Indeed, those in control firmly believe themselves the only ones competent to effect change.

Although elsewhere clearly identifying with the weak, Jesus in these parables, with greater or lesser intensity, allows his listeners to identify with the overlord, render him trustworthy, and collude with him in making a scapegoat of the weaker. (Among his authentic longer parables, the single exception to this pattern is the Good Samaritan, and the single challenge to it is the Unjust Judge.) Such blaming comes easily—because the under-lings are indeed blameworthy. They have murdered, cringed, grumbled, choked, and wasted. Already confounded by such negative behavior, listen-ers' incipient awareness of long histories of imposed injustice is decisively dismissed by the overlords' self-serving declarations, which is where each story ends.

In this way of reading, these narratives with uncanny accuracy repli-cate how elites of every empire, then and now, persistently eviscerate our awareness of what is really going on. As are persons subjected to relentless dominance, we as listeners are also rendered vulnerable to such controlling definitions. If we agree with the perspectives of the entitled superior, if we accept as accurate *his* descriptions of what is going on, we fail to suspect that fundamental responsibilities for the parable's tragedy rest with him. We then join the overlord in solving the parable's difficulties simply by blaming his far more vulnerable—and obviously blameworthy—subordinate.

However, what these parables hold out as seeming resolutions provid-ed by the powerful—the landlord's retribution, the talent master's praising, the vineyard owner's generosity, the releasing master's punishing, the rich man's commending, the father's forgiving, the householder's giving, and the judge's vindicating—on careful examination turn out to resolve nothing at all. Indeed, when the consequences of the overlord's actions are looked at closely, listeners discover a continuation in even more hidden ways of the unjust structures already in place. As before, farmers are left defrauded. Slaves are still demeaned. Laborers continue in poverty. A neglected man-ager is abandoned to self-defeating scheming. Sons are blocked in their development. An unsustainable generosity still deprives the poor. A widow and her community remain bereft of law.

Here may be discerned the moment when these parables, in silent invitation, turn toward their listeners. The focus is now on us, for now *we* are charged with deciding what is going on. Having subjected us to an astonishing re-creation of the strategies of ancient—and modern—elites, having drawn us to give authority to the parable's heralded superiors, Jesus then steps back and entrusts to his listeners the work of disentangling these misleading definitions of the overlords.

Gradually we begin to realize that we as listeners *are the only ones left* who can do this difficult work. We are the only ones positioned to enter more deeply into the experience of those subjected to power. We are given the task of overcoming the bias, the pain, the muting of sequence, and the perversity that Jesus has so deftly enclosed in his stories. We are the only ones able to suspect the ultimately tragic trajectories of the powerful. Jesus provides us with the opportunity to discover both how extensively the superiors have misled us and how the supposedly reprehensible subordinates are, if not heroes, then persons forced to struggle with the endless distortions foisted on them during lifetimes of being dominated.

Once we release the superior character from the constricting role of representing God, once we question his behaviors with the same intensity we bring to examining those of his subordinate, we in the First World empower these narratives to interrogate the untoward consequences of our own privilege. Here we start to move away from simply listening to becoming active participants. By drawing us into this work, Jesus embodies how his God wants *us* to be the ones to struggle across the seemingly impenetrable barriers of dominance and so be with and for each other.

The Work of Parable Listeners: Part 2

If readers are willing to entertain these perspectives, they are then positioned to realize how most modern interpretations of these stories (1) have transformed the economic perpetrator into a theological exemplar, and (2) have shifted the locus of the kingdom's advent away from a chronically conflicted present into an altogether certain future. (Concerning this move, someone has observed, "Utopia is the end of politics.") It is hard to imagine a more effective way of subverting what Jesus was about, or a more efficient way of relieving listeners of difficult work.

The enormity of this betrayal may be measured by the work it takes to undo it. At its foundation such work involves our re-vising, our looking again, at how we perceive the perpetrator of economic injustice. Such a change in perspective enables us to discover openings within a seemingly impermeable parable frame, which in turn allow us to expand the options available to our decision making.

These openings, difficult to locate, are discovered by paying close attention to the truly puzzling behaviors of the underlings. Why would vulnerable tenant farmers murder the son? Why would a fearful slave bury the talent? Why would misused agricultural workers anticipate an equitable generosity? Why would a released slave cashier a minor colleague? Why would an astute manager compromise his entire security? Why would an isolated son waste his sole resource? Why would the chronically destitute trust a precipitate generosity? Why would a powerless widow provoke a dangerous retaliation? By engaging in each of these behaviors the underling seems certain to be shattered.

When the actions of these underlings become perplexing, when questions about their behavior do not yield obvious answers, we may suspect the disguised impact of disowned violence from the overlords. Those underlings insistently overwhelmed by their superiors' dominance (and such dominance can be exercised through generosity as well as through controlling) eventually lose their ability to describe what is happening to them. In the end these subordinates are reduced to communicating through reprehensible, self-defeating actions. Parable listeners, like archeologists, are called upon to dig through layers of such debilitating distortion in order to reach long-buried evidence of a more fundamental violence. It is hard work. We are tasked with uncovering how each parable's tragedy—the tenants' murdering, both slaves' being cast out, the laborers' bitterness, the manager's self-destructiveness, the younger son's humiliation, the coming disappointment of the impoverished guests, and the widow's empty vindication—is the consequence of an earlier coercion.

Jesus invites us to detect, etched across each underling's blameworthy behavior, the indistinct but unmistakable outline of the overlord's prior domination. The tenants' murdering is in response to the landowner's imperialism. The slave's burying is in response to the master's exploiting. The laborers' grumbling is in response to the owner's shaming. The slave's choking is in response to the master's controlling. The manager's wasting is in response to the rich man's neglect. The son's scattering is in response to the father's need to be needed. The approaching disappointment of the destitute is a coming response to the householder's preoccupation with respect. The widow's battering is in response to the judge's breathtaking self-centeredness. What has brought about each underling's seemingly reprehensible behavior, resulting in their own ongoing debasement, is the previous violence of the overlord. In this way Jesus consistently locates evidence of the superior's bankrupt integrity inside the untoward responses of the subordinate.

This thesis—that a prior, disguised violence in the superior emerges in the contours of the subordinate's blameworthy behavior—becomes less persuasive across the course of inquiry into these eight parables. Put another way, except for the Unjust Judge, violence in the superior becomes harder and harder to locate as one proceeds through each parable. More obvious is the violence of the landowner towards the farmers his social class has dispossessed, of the talent master towards the masses he exploits, and of the vineyard owner towards the workers he deprives. As the inquiry into all eight parables progresses, less open to suspicion is the violence of the slave master towards his unforgiving slave or the violence of the rich man towards his delinquent manager.

However, to label as violent the prodigal father's behavior toward his profligate son or that of the householder in relation to his impoverished guests is clearly less convincing. Needed are more subtle terms able to capture the distortions imposed by an over ambitious generosity—terms that comprehend the damage done by the father when he entices his son toward humiliation, or terms that grasp the coming disillusionment engineered by the householder when he offers a largess he is unlikely to be able to sustain.

Only listeners are positioned to recognize in their entirety these larger sequences—sequences initiated but never acknowledged by the overlord, then inarticulately enacted by the underling, and, finally, rehidden by the overlord's self-justifying proclamations. While Jesus lures us to suspect these sequences, he in no way *makes* us go there. He allows us, but never requires us, to expand the range of our inquiry. He draws us, but never compels us, to engage difficulties that both complicate and enhance our ability to understand. The transformational element in these stories is here located in the aroused scope and depth of listeners' efforts to grasp what is truly going on.

Control Leading to Irony

The profound levels reached by Jesus's nonconfrontational approach are astounding. He does not demand. He proffers, disguises, and then lures. He allows us, if we wish, to arrive at understandings that fit readily within established patterns of dominance and submission while all the time offering us alternatives. We can take such prior interpretations and go our way, believing ourselves satisfied. Or we can work to discover how these brief parables encompass lengthy histories leading to extraordinarily painful ironies.[4]

4. A way into the irony is to grasp the full sweep of each narrative's lengthy sequence. In schematic terms (a) early on, most often before the parable begins, the oppressor oppresses; (b) in response, the oppressed become oppressors (either of others or of themselves), thus mirroring the original oppressor; (c) the original oppressor in turn attacks

Consistently, these ironies focus on the powerful. Because he so much wants to believe himself within the law, a landlord exposes his son to lethal lawlessness. An exploiting slave master is incensed that one of his exploited slaves does not follow his example. A vineyard owner sincerely believes his momentary generosity overcomes his chronic depriving. An imperious slave master imprisons his slave because the slave imitates him. A rich man, full of neglect towards a competent subordinate, cashiers him for neglect. A loving father fails to suspect that his undisciplined generosity toward his undisciplined son may in fact undermine any chance the son has to develop some discipline of his own. Because he so much wants to control through his generosity the lost recognition he seeks, a householder fails to evaluate the impact of his participation in fostering the impoverishment of the poor. A seemingly self-sufficient judge demeans a reliance on community that in fact constitutes the foundation of his independence.

Lodged within these ironies may be an answer to a puzzling question: why does Jesus mimic, in the way he creates his narratives, various forms of domination? To answer such a question sensitively, we must first suppose that Jesus was not addressing his fellow peasants directly so much as he was describing to them those persons whose privilege was making their lives miserable. Here we may suspect that important members of Jesus's intended audience were those ethically sensitive but nonetheless enthralled members of the retainer class pulled simultaneously in opposite directions. On the one hand, they inhabited spheres of status and profit derived from servicing aristocratic greed. On the other hand, they struggled with multiple betrayals—of divine intention, of their own belonging, and of the great numbers of their fellow Jews who were looking to them for support. By creating narratives in which the powerful not only impose their definitions but also offer their rewards, Jesus evokes precisely the world in which these retainers lived. With the ensuing ironies, he then lures these same hearers to penetrate the seductive facade of their seemingly normative environment.

---

the oppressed for becoming oppressors. There are variations at this final stage. In the case of the tenants, the oppressor, the landlord, fails to attack his oppressed tenants after they themselves have become oppressors. In the case of the prodigal, the oppressing father falsely forgives his oppressed son, who is attacking himself. Finally, in the case of the talents, the oppressing slave master attacks his oppressed slave for having resisted becoming an oppressor. (This overarching schema is least persuasive for the parable of the poor and the householder. For it to apply there, one must imagine a future disillusionment and imposed depression among the poor when the householder's ability to sustain his generosity flags.)

He steadily draws them to sense the dangers in what they have embraced. These are the same persons who read this book.

Empathy Leading to Access

In the present approach, the primary mode of access to these parables is through empathy. To be empathic means to put yourself in the shoes of the other, whether poor or powerful, and to imagine how they might think and feel. Empathy does not mean agreement. We humans are most ready to grasp the inner perspectives, however problematic, of those we love. Sustaining such enabled empathy is far easier than being deeply present when differences in power provoke degrading forces that can only be experienced as hateful. The empathic observer, when reaching to understand what the other is trying to do, may well not approve. Empathy involves comprehending how alien behaviors, however puzzling or distasteful or even intolerable, are from the participants' point of view the best options conceivable.

Using such a strategy, the parable listener engages in a slowly expanding, stepwise process. You the listener are drawn initially to focus on the maladaptive responses of the underling. You first see him as a miscreant. You then discover that his behaviors are not simply of his own making but represent reactions shaped by the overlord's prior controlling. By feeling into the underling's smoldering humiliation, you finally gain access to the corrupting behaviors of the overlord. Only later are you able to reach into the overlord's distorted inner experience.

Difficult as it is for contemporary listeners to grasp what it is like to be the underling, it is far harder for us to empathize with the perspectives of the overlord. When we present-day listeners try to empathize with the parable's superior character, we encounter difficulties equal to what we experience when we try to engage the varied forms of modern malaise. We confront not a series of steps but a chasm. Because of the imbalance in power, the two domains—of the oppressed and of the oppressor—are widely divergent. Where the underling experiences directly the onslaughts of domination, the overlord has far more resources to hide any inner pain or doubt both from others and from himself. He offers few footholds to the inquirer trying to climb the sheer cliffs of his confident facade. By virtue of the profound self-deceptions essential to his access to power, the overlord, beyond most observation and out of reach even of his own awareness, becomes the self-isolated enabler of his eventual deprivation.

Jesus focuses in these parables on the vulnerabilities inherent in economic and political power. Listeners can learn to see what both overlord and underling cannot see, namely, how the overlord's control has and will continue to reap loss. By achieving this perspective, such listeners must then struggle with a pervasive tension, inherent both in the parable and in modern global distress, between short-term gain and long-term loss. Where is the benefit in trying to construe your unlawfulness as lawful? How is it profitable to make a disproportional profit? What do you achieve when you try to convince others that you are a good person—when you are not? What do you gain by coercing the allegiance of people who hate you? What is the benefit in convincing yourself you are in control—when you are not? How do these behaviors continue to make sense? How is it you cannot see where you are going?

Because he so believes in what he is doing, the overlord remains unaware to the very end of the ironies embedded in his self-inflicted loss. No matter how imminent the looming tragedy, the overlord's behavior, in his own eyes, continues to make sense. Even after tragedy strikes, often well after the parable ends, he remains certain he is right. Listeners alone are left to experience the needlessness of the pain inflicted by the overlord, not only on his underlings, but on himself. Here, in this way of understanding, listeners find themselves sitting down beside the divine and sharing in the immense sadness of God.

Empathy across Distance and across Time: Contemporary Issues

By their pervasive provision of irony, hidden inside hierarchies of privilege, these parables demonstrate profoundly the perils inherent in the possession of power. We benefit from equally seductive cultures of dominance. In these ancient interpersonal tragedies we can discover modern global analogues—where the powerful still control the powerless, and where others of us, immersed as we are in privilege, continue to side with control.

Within each contemporary global conflict are those who dominate and those who are dominated. The ones dominating have over time created impersonal structures that insulate them from having to feel the suffering of those whom they deprive. Thus those who collect income from stocks do not have to know how much is derived from unfair labor practices or from undermining the public's health. Thus the Wall Street executives who have carefully designed subprime mortgages keep their distance from the suffering they have inflicted, for example, on a young teacher in the inner city who is evicted with his family into the street. Thus the politician who enables, for a price, the shifting of billions in state pension funds into hedge funds does not have to feel the angst of a retired secretary seeing her fixed income subjected to unregulated risk taking. Thus First World bankers do not have to feel their betrayal of Third World children, whose entire future is destroyed by the draining power of floating interest rates.

We have difficulty grasping in full the complexities of modern global events partly because we cannot possibly comprehend the inner experience of each in the multitude of individual players. We are instead limited to observing broad themes. Here is where these parables intersect with and become entry points for comprehending particularities in the broad sweep of modern distress. Here we are isolated with only two persons. They in turn become a proving ground for extending and deepening our awareness both of others' experience and our own.

A subset of our difficulty in empathizing across impersonal distance is our difficulty in empathizing across interpersonal time. Here the issue is not differences in social class but rather the gulf between the born and the unborn. Only one side has a voice. For example, in a world of avoidable climate change, we who are alive can simply refuse to hear the still-inaudible cries of millions of unborn climate refugees. In our current calculating of the costs, the massive weight of this coming despair has yet to be placed in the balance. Here the parable listener, by paying closer attention to individual experience, is called upon to fill in that void, heft that burden, and dump it on the scale.

Comprehending the gradual unfolding of parable sequence, of that long progression of interacting events lying behind the immediate actions and reactions of the two parable participants, becomes an effective practice arena for empathizing across distance and time. These parables invite us to keep on asking, before this happened, what happened? After this happens, what is going to happen? Such inquiry counters the overwhelming investment those who dominate have in erasing from our awareness the devastating consequences of their long-standing control.

Modern analogues to ancient counterparts invariably involve parallel histories of violently assumed privilege—leading to analogous reactions of inarticulate violence among the oppressed. Resisting both forms of domination, Jesus invites us to enter with him into the cadres of the nonviolent. In turn his parables, in their fundamental structure, embody this same nonviolence. His narratives themselves are skeptical about the effectiveness of coercion to induce positive change. In the way they function, they do not coercively—that is, decisively—expose the consequences of reliance on coercion. Instead they employ indirection, entrusting to their listeners, to the extent listeners are willing, the essential work of perceiving their tragedy and transforming their violence.

We are invited to enter into the despairing experience of the underlings, to become present both to this one's unfortunate identification with the aggressor and to that one's courageous ability to have some excruciatingly limited effect on the overlord. We are challenged to understand the ultimately self-defeating nature of the overlord's passionate dedication to control. We are summoned to wrestle with the remarkable self-deceptions essential to his accumulation of power. Such avenues of awareness become a major resource for imagining how the God of Jesus stands, now as then, with both the powerless and the powerful in their every attempt, however limited, to mitigate the distressing course of events.

The ways we grasp these parables can help us see better the ways we grasp contemporary issues. For example, do we resonate with the experience of the underling as well as we do with that of the overlord? Conversely, do we ponder the perspective of the overlord as deeply as we do that of the underling? For us in the First World, are we as aware of how much our violence provokes the hatred of others as we are of how much we hate the violence in the way others respond to us? Do we sense how our dominance can so infiltrate and condition those we dominate that they come to imitate us? Do we grasp how much our charity, when used to mask the extent of our control, can enrage? Do we treat the experienced history of strangers with the same awareness we invest in our own? Do we look to the safety and comfort of our children's children's children with the same passion we devote to our own?

Since, if we are to enter them more fully, these parables steadfastly require their listeners to exercise empathy, readers may become open to the idea that Jesus conceived of his God as the locus of a consummate empathy. Just as we humans empathize with those nearest to us, we are drawn to imagine how the God of Jesus rejoices and weeps with everyone, profoundly, everywhere and throughout all time. How his God embraces the vast ranges of benevolence and malevolence in *all* of human experience, enclosing as it does both painful self-awareness and tragic self-deception. To follow such a God is to enter the kingdom of God.

The Luring of Jesus and the Longing of God

When we probe the question, what do these parables ask of us? one answer might be, they ask us to enter into them, and then to go further in—and then to go even further in. Among the questions these further penetrations expose is, How does Jesus's unusual manner of teaching embody his understanding of God?

Here we discover two underlying and necessarily complementary perspectives. (1) God will not intervene. (2) God depends on us to intervene. In parallel fashion, in his parables Jesus does not make declarations. Instead he invites our collaboration. He looks to us to respond. Without our participation, his parables are stillborn. Not only does he rely on us, he draws us further in. The more we seek, the more his parables give back. In this realm of open-ended reciprocity our initiative is needed, respected, and rewarded. We can go in as far, dive as deeply, and climb as high as we wish, all the time accompanied, but all the time given the freedom, whenever we want it, to turn aside.

One underlying thrust of this book is to propose that

it is precisely these nonconfrontational, noncoercive, ambiguous, and entrusting characteristics of Jesus's way of telling stories,

both inviting and then depending on his listeners to exercise their own initiative,

in turn located at the very center of his authentic teaching,

that compellingly supports the proposition that the historical Jesus did *not* envision,

however prominent such an expectation was all around him,

the imminent coming of an externally imposed, decisively transforming, divine intervention into human affairs.

This book's approach understands Jesus instead to be locating some of the kingdom's coming, some of the advent of God's longing for us humans, inside the very ways we choose to grasp his parables. The only way into these narratives is through a disciplined empathy. Subverted is any attempt more directly to capture decisive meaning. Opening up to us, then, is the possibility that these narratives may be understood not as stories containing hidden messages to be deciphered but rather as histories containing distorted sequences to be experienced.

The ways Jesus lures us to understand his parables suggests the ways he understood his God to rule. God does not demand. God does not impose. God does not intervene. Instead, God waits. God provides possibilities. God entrusts to us the work of choosing. In turn we can listen or not, respond or not. However if, in the midst of all the tragedy, we fail to grasp the profound desire of God for the *entire* creation to thrive, then the endless cycle of the oppressed becoming oppressors persists. Violence continues to create victims, and those victims continue to create violence. If we lose hold of God's passionate embrace, all that changes is our growing capacity to destroy. The lengthy sequences enclosed in these parables each traverse portions of this endless cycle's perimeters. At its boundary the God of Jesus waits, holding out her arms, longing for us to break through.

[Jesus] told them many things in parables, saying,

Listen . . . listen . . . see . . .
perceive . . . hear . . . listen . . .
understand . . . listen . . . understand . . .
look . . . perceive . . . hear . . . look . . .
listen . . . understand . . . see . . . hear . . .
—Matt 13:3–16 (NRSV, abridged)

APPENDIX

Parable Boundaries

IT IS IMPORTANT TO distinguish the boundaries between, on the one hand, those portions of the texts of Jesus's parables that are closer to how he actually spoke them, and, on the other hand, the contexts in which later Gospel editors placed them. The three examples offered here demonstrate the remarkable disjunctions that have occurred between the more original forms of the authentic parables and their surrounding Gospel contexts.

One way to identify these boundaries is to notice the intrusion into these parables' texts of various levels of divine violence. A model for this seemingly inevitable process may be found in a condensed form in an Apocrypha narrative created in response to persecution, which in turn provides an analogue to the persecution of early Jewish Christians around the time the Gospels were written.

Composed around 124 BCE, 2 Maccabees 7 recounts events that take place during the reign of the Greek-speaking Seleucid king Antiochus IV (175–164 BCE). The king is attempting to impose Greek customs and institutions on the Jews; in this segment he is trying to force seven Jewish brothers to eat the flesh of swine. Rather than comply they choose to endure torture and die. The author's imagining of God's response to this travesty moves quickly across three stages.

Stage 1: Powerless suffering is coupled with God's *vindicating* the oppressed. As the first son dies a horrific death, the brothers say, "The Lord God is watching over us and in truth has compassion on us . . . " (v. 6).

Stage 2: Powerless suffering is coupled with God's *vindictiveness* towards the oppressor. As the fourth son approaches death, he says, "One cannot but choose to die at the hands of mortals and to cherish the hope

God gives of being raised again by him. But for you there will be no resurrection to life!" (v. 14).

Stage 3: Powerless suffering is coupled with God's *violence* towards the oppressor. The fifth son, horribly tortured and about to die, looks at the king and says, "Because you have authority among mortals, though you also are mortal, you do what you please. But do not think that God has forsaken our people. Keep on, and see how his mighty power will torture you and your descendants" (vv. 15–17).

In the span of eleven verses, the author, full of anger on behalf of the oppressed, is moving dangerously close to becoming an oppressor—because once you start imagining a violent God, you are at risk of becoming violent yourself.

There is a readily understandable rationale for this insidious increase in religiously based violence. (1) I am oppressed. (2) I am enraged. (3) I direct my rage at those who have abused me. (4) I further imagine others who will abuse me. (5) Then, in religious terms, I imagine a devil orchestrating such abuse. (6) Then I imagine a God who can control that devil. (7) I can then split the world into good and bad. I can divide my fellow human beings into "sheep" and "goats" and can make the "goats" part of the devil. (8) I can then in my imagination make my vindicating God into a vindictive God who exiles "goats," or into a violent God who tortures and kills "goats." (9) If I ever get enough power, I can then, in the name of my God, torture and kill. I, the oppressed, have become an oppressor.

Specific evidence for parts of the above sequence can be found in the Gospel contexts for three of the parables discussed in this book—contexts that differ in important ways from the parables themselves. Readers need to know that between forty to eighty years separate the spoken parables from their later Gospel contexts. Without awareness of such boundaries, readers may assume that Jesus spoke not only the parables but also the surrounding dissonant commentary.

Here are descriptions of the serious misfits that have developed between each of three parables and their later Gospel contexts.

(1) The parable of the Unjust Judge (with its context of God's *vindicating*). If you look only at the parable itself, you will see that nowhere in that narrative is there any hint of external resolution; no one enters from the outside to rescue the beleaguered widow or to discipline the self-centered judge.

However, immediately following the parable is a resolution imposed by the Gospel editor, one that is at odds with the parable's carefully crafted blocking of outside intervention: "And the Lord said, 'Listen to what the unjust judge says. And will not God grant justice to his chosen ones who cry to him day and night. Will he delay long in helping them? I tell you, he will quickly grant justice to them'" (Luke 18:6–8 NRSV).

Underlying Luke's language is the presumption of an established community of believers living under duress. There were, obviously, no such communities at the time Jesus told his stories. Described here is the first stage in the sequence laid out so clearly in 2 Maccabees 7. When people are under duress, they cry out for help. They imagine an all-powerful God will vindicate them.

(2) The parable of the Talents (with its context of God's *vindictiveness*). Many readers of this parable, influenced by Matthew's allegorical understanding of it, assume that the master who gives out the talents is a figure for God or Jesus. Jesus goes away and then comes back—and at the final judgment evaluates what his servants have done with their God-given talents. In response to the third slave Matthew has the master say, "As for this worthless slave, throw him into the outer darkness, where there will be weeping and gnashing of teeth" (Matt 25:30 NRSV).

Matthew's giving over the parable's meaning to the master's final judgment cannot possibly match how the original hearers would have evaluated this man. They know who he is; they know how he stole their land. They would certainly not endow such a person with the capacity to judge justly but would instead identify him as criminal. However, Matthew's allegorical context has Jesus, as the final judge, separating the sheep from the goats and throwing away the goats. Now we are in the realm of a vindictive God and fast on our way to imagining a violent God.

(3) The Wicked Tenants (with its context of God's *violence*). If you contrast Mark's version of this parable with a probably more original version in the Gospel of Thomas, it becomes clear how much Mark, writing forty years after Jesus taught, has transformed Jesus's original story to fit his allegorical interpretation, namely, that the wounded slaves represent the prophets and the beloved son is Jesus himself.

In order to enhance his allegory, Mark is willing to put violence into the mouth of Jesus. "What will the owner of the vineyard [that is, God] do? He will come and destroy the tenants [that is, the Jewish leaders] and give the vineyard to others [that is, to the Jewish Christians]" (Mark 12:9

NRSV). We have now entered the realm of a violent God. While it was only incipiently dangerous when Christians were powerless, once Western Christianity attained empire-level dominance, Mark's allegorical interpretation eventually became an intolerable justification for the Holocaust.

Bibliography

Alter, Robert. *Genesis: Translation and Commentary*. New York: Norton, 1996.

Appelbaum, Shimon. "Economic Life in Palestine." In *The Jewish People in the First Century: Historical Geography, Political History, Social, Cultural and Religious Life and Institutions*, edited by S. Safrai and M. Stern in cooperation with D. Flusser and W. C. van Unnik, 631–700. Compendium rerum iudaicarum ad Novum Testamentum 2. Philadelphia: Fortress, 1976.

Arndt, William F., and F. Wilbur Gingrich. *A Greek-English Lexicon of the New Testament and Other Early Christian Literature*. Chicago: University of Chicago Press, 1957.

Awad, Hassan Juma'a, and the Iraqi Federation of Oil Unions. "Letter to the Shareholders of ExxonMobil and Chevron Coproations." Presented May 30, 2008. Published by U. S. Labor against the War on May 28, 2008. https://www.indybay.org/newsitems/2008/05/25/18502090.php/.

Bailey, Kenneth E. *Jacob and the Prodigal: How Jesus Retold Israel's Story*. Downers Grove, IL: InterVarsity, 2003.

———. *Poet and Peasant and Through Peasant Eyes. A Literary-Cultural Approach to the Parables in Luke*. Combined ed. Grand Rapids, Michigan: Eerdmans, 1984.

Bartlett, Donald L., and James B. Steele. *The Betrayal of the American Dream*. New York: Public Affairs, 2012.

Berenson, Bernard. *The Passionate Sightseer: From the Diaries 1947 to 1956*. London: Thames & Hudson, 1960.

Booth, Wayne C. *The Rhetoric of Irony*. Chicago: University of Chicago Press, 1974.

Borg, Marcus J. "A Temperate Case for a Non-Eschatological Jesus." *Foundations & Facets Forum* 2,3 (1986) 81–102. Reprinted in Borg, *Jesus in Contemporary Scholarship*. Valley Forge, PA: Trinity, 1994.

Borg, Marcus J., and N. T. Wright. *The Meaning of Jesus: Two Visions*. San Francisco: HarperSanFrancisco, 1998.

Breech, James. *The Silence of Jesus: The Authentic Voice of the Historical Man*. Philadelphia: Fortress, 1983.

Brown, Francis et al. *A Hebrew English Lexicon of the Old Testament*. Oxford: Oxford University Press, 1957.

Bush, George W. "Bush Asserts Progress in Iraq." CQ Transcripts Wire. Post Politics. *Washington Post*, March 27, 2008. http://www.washingtonpost.com/wp-dyn/content/article/2008/03/27/AR2008032701738.html/

———. "Bush Remarks on Iraq War and Terrorism." CQ Transcripts. Post Politics. *Washington Post*, March 19, 2008. http://www.washingtonpost.com/wp-dyn/content/article/2008/03/19/AR2008031901083.html/.

———. "President's Radio Address, March 22, 2003." *Public Papers of the Presidents: George W. Bush*; 2003, Book 1. *The American Presidency Project*. http://www.presidency.ucsb.edu/ws/?pid=25127/.

Cardinal, Ernesto, ed. *The Gospel in Solentiname*. 4 vols. Maryknoll, NY: Orbis, 1982.

Carlson, Jeffrey, and Robert A. Ludwig, eds. *Jesus and Faith. A Conversation on the Work of John Dominic Crossan*. Maryknoll, NY: Orbis, 1994.

Carney, Thomas F. *The Shape of the Past: Models of Antiquity*. Lawrence, KS: Coronado, 1975.

Chilton, Bruce. "The Kingdom of God in Recent Discussion." In *Studying the Historical Jesus: Evaluations of the State of Current Research*, edited by Bruce Chilton and Craig A. Evans, 255–80. New Testament Tools and Studies 19. Leiden: Brill, 1994.

Coll, Steve. *Private Empire: ExxonMobil and American Power*. New York: Penguin, 2012.

Crossan, John Dominic. *The Birth of Christianity: Discovering What Happened in the Years after the Execution of Jesus*. San Francisco: HarperSanFrancisco, 1998.

———. *The Historical Jesus: The Life of a Mediterranean Peasant*. San Francisco: HarperSanFrancisco, 1991.

Dash, Eric. "Federal Report Faults Banks on Huge Bonuses." *New York Times*, July 23, 2010, A3. http://www.nytimes.com/2010/07/23/business/23pay.html?_r=0/.

Davies, W. D. *The Territorial Dimension of Judaism*. Berkeley: University of California Press, 1982.

DeBoer, Martinus C. "Ten Thousand Talents? Matthew's Interpretation and the Redaction of the Parable of the Unforgiving Servant (Matt. 18:23–35)." *Catholic Biblical Quarterly* 50 (1988) 214–32.

Drury, John. *The Parables in the Gospels*. New York: Crossroad, 1985.

Duling, Denis C. "The Jesus Movement and Social Network Analysis (Part I: The Spatial Network)." *Biblical Theology Bulletin* 29 (2000) 156–75.

Edwards, Douglas. "The Socio-Economic and Cultural Ethos of the Lower Galilee in the First Century: Implications for the Nascent Jesus Movement." In *Galilee in Late Antiquity*, edited by Lee I. Levine, 53–73. New York: Jewish Theological Seminary of America, 1992.

Eikenberry, Karl. Memo to Hillary Clinton, November 6, 2009. http://documents.nytimes.com/eikenberry-s-memos-on-the-strategy-in-afghanistan/.

Fiensy, David A. *The Social History of Palestine in the Herodian Period: The Land is Mine*. Studies in the Bible and Early Christianity 20. Lewiston, NY: Mellon, 1991.

Folger, Tim. "Rising Seas." *National Geographic Magazine*. September, 2013, 30–59. http://ngm.nationalgeographic.com/2013/09/rising-seas/folger-text.

Fortna, Robert T. "Reading Jesus' Parable of the Talents through Underclass Eyes." *Forum* 8,3/4 (1992) 211–28.

Freyne, Sean. *Galilee from Alexander the Great to Hadrian, 323 B.C.E. to 145 C.E.: A Study in Second Temple Judaism*. University of Notre Dame Center for the Study of Judaism and Christianity in Antiquity 5. Wilmington, DE: Glazier, 1980.

———. *Galilee, Jesus, and the Gospels: Literary Approaches and Historical Investigations*. Philadelphia: Fortress, 1988.

———. "The Geography, Politics, and Economics of Galilee and the Quest for the Historical Jesus." In *Studying the Historical Jesus: Evaluations of the State of Current Research*, edited by Bruce Chilton and Craig A. Evans, 75–112. New Testament Tools and Studies 19. Leiden: Brill, 1994.

Funk, Robert W., Bernard Brandon Scott, and James R. Butts, eds. *The Parables of Jesus. A Red Letter Edition*. Sonoma, CA: Polebridge, 1988.

Goodman, Amy. "New Iraq Oil Law to Open Iraq's Oil Reserves to Western Companies." *Democracy Now: The War and Peace Report*. February 20, 2007. http://www.democracynow.org/2007/2/20/new_iraq_oil_law_to_open.

Goodman, Martin. "The First Jewish Revolt: Social Conflict and the Problem of Debt." *Journal of Jewish Studies* 33 (1982) 417–27.

Greenspan, Alan. *The Age of Turbulence: Adventures in a New World*. New York: Penguin, 2007.

Hanson, K. C., and Douglas E. Oakman. *Palestine in the Time of Jesus: Social Structures and Social Conflicts*. 2nd ed. Minneapolis: Fortress, 2008.

Herzog, William R. II. *Parables as Subversive Speech: Jesus as Pedagogue of the Oppressed*. Louisville: Westminster John Knox, 1994.

Horsley, Richard A. *Archaeology, History, and Society in Galilee*. Valley Forge, PA: Trinity, 1996.

———. *Galilee: History, Politics, People*. Valley Forge, PA: Trinity, 1996.

Intergovernmental Panel on Climate Change. *Climate Change 2014: Synthesis Report*. Contribution of Working Groups I, II and III to the Fifth Assessment Report of the Intergovernmental Panel on Climate Change. Edited by R. K. Pachauri and L. A. Meyer. Geneva: Intergovernmental Panel on Climate Change, 2015.

Jeremias, Joachim. *The Parables of Jesus*. 2nd rev. ed. Translated by S. H. Hooke. New York: Scribner, 1972.

Kähler, Christoph. *Jesu Gleichnesse als Poesie und Therapie: Versuch eines integrativen Zugangs zum kommunikativen Aspekt von Gleichnissen Jesu*. Wissenschaftliche Untersuchungen zum Neuen Testament 78. Tübingen: Mohr/Siebek, 1995.

Kautsky, John H. *The Politics of Aristocratic Empires*. Chapel Hill: University of North Carolina Press, 1982.

Kaylor, R. David. *Jesus the Prophet: His Vision of the Kingdom on Earth*. Louisville: Westminster John Knox, 1994.

Kee, Howard Clark. "Early Christianity in the Galilee: Reassessing the Evidence from the Gospels." In *The Galilee in Late Antiquity*, edited by Lee I. Levine, 3–22. New York: Jewish Theological Seminary of America, 1992.

Kinzer, Stephen. *All the Shah's Men: An American Coup and the Roots of Middle East Terror*. New York: Wiley, 2003.

———. *Overthrow: America's Century of Regime Change from Hawaii to Iraq*. New York: Holt, 2006.

Klare, Michael T. *Blood and Oil: The Dangers and Consequences of America's Growing Dependency on Imported Petroleum*. New York: Holt, 2004.

Kloppenborg, John S. *The Tenants in the Vineyard: Ideology, Economics, and Agrarian Conflict in Jewish Palestine*. Wissenschaftliche Untersuchungen zum Neuen Testament 195. Tübingen: Mohr/Siebeck, 2006.

Leibowitz, Nehama. *Studies in Bereshīt (Genesis), in the Context of Ancient and Modern Jewish Bible Commentary*. Translated and adapted from the Hebrew by Aryeh Newman. Jerusalem: World Zionist Organization, Department for Torah Education and Culture, 1985.

Lenski, Gerhard E. *Power and Privilege: A Theory of Social Stratification*. New York: McGraw-Hill, 1966.

Mackey, Sandra. *The Reckoning: Iraq and the Legacy of Saddam Hussein*. New York: Norton, 2002.

Mayer, Jane. "Contact Sport." *New Yorker*, February 16 and 23, 2004, 80–91.

McKibben, Bill. "Global Warming's Terrifying New Math: Three Simple Numbers That Add up to Global Catastrophe—and That Make Clear Who the Real Enemy Is." *Rolling Stone* (August 12, 2012) 52–60.

Meeks, Wayne A. et al., eds. *The Harper Collins Study Bible: New Revised Standard Version*. New York: HarperCollins, 1993.

Meyers, Eric M. "Roman Sepphoris in Light of New Archaeological Research." In *The Galilee in Late Antiquity*, edited by Lee I. Levine, 321–38. New York: Jewish Theological Seminary of America, 1992.

Miller, Peter. "Weather Gone Wild." *National Geographic*, September 2012, 30–53.

Miller, Robert J., ed. *The Apocalyptic Jesus: A Debate*. Santa Rosa, CA: Polebridge, 2001.

———, ed. *The Complete Gospels: Annotated Scholar's Version*. Rev. and exp. ed. Sonoma, CA: Polebridge, 1994.

Milmo Calhan et al. "In Olympic Year, China Urged to Use Its Influence in Darfur." *Independent*, February 13, 2008. http://www.independent.co.uk/news/world/asia/in-olympic-year-china-urged-to-use-its-influence-in-darfur-782011.html

Moe-Lobeda, Cynthia D. *Resisting Structural Evil: Love as Ecological-Economic Vocation*. Minneapolis: Fortress, 2013.

Moyo, Dambisa F. *Winner Take All: China's Race for Resources and What It Means for the World*. New York: Basic Books, 2012.

Muecke, Douglas C. *Irony and the Ironic*. 2nd ed. London: Methuen, 1982.

Muttitt, Gregg. "Crude Designs: The Rip-Off of Iraq's Oil Wealth." http://www.globalpolicy.org/security/oil/2005/crudedesigns.htm.

———. *Fuel on the Fire: Oil and Politics in Occupied Iraq*. New York: New Press, 2012.

Neusner, Jacob. *From Politics to Piety: The Emergence of Pharisaic Piety*. 2nd ed. 1979. Reprinted, Eugene, OR: Wipf & Stock, 2003.

New, Mark G. et al. "Four Degrees and Beyond: The Potential for a Global Temperature Increase of Four Degrees and Its Implications." *Philosophical Transactions*. Series A. London: Royal Society (January 13, 2011).

Ngũgĩ wa Thiong'o. *Devil on the Cross*. Translated by the author. African Writers Series 200. London: Heinemann, 1982.

Oakman, Douglas E. "The Buying Power of Two Denarii: A Comment on Luke 10:35." *Forum* 3,4 (1987) 33–38. Reprinted in Oakman, *Jesus and the Peasants*, 40–45. Matrix: The Bible in Mediterranean Context 4. Eugene, OR: Cascade Books, 2008.

———. *Jesus and the Economic Questions of His Day*. Studies in the Bible and Early Christianity 8. Lewiston, NY: Mellon, 1986.

Oreskes, Naomi, and Erik M. Conway. *The Collapse of Western Civilization: A View from the Future*. New York: Columbia University Press, 2014.

———. *Merchants of Doubt: How a Handful of Scientists Obscured the Truth on Issues from Tobacco Smoke to Global Warming*. New York: Bloomsbury, 2010.

Patey, Luke Anthony. *A Complex Reality: The Strategic Behavior of Corporations and the New Wars in Sudan*. Copenhagen: Danish Institute for International Studies, 2006. http://www.diis.dk/.

———. *State Rules: Oil Companies and Armed Conflict in Sudan*. Copenhagen: Danish Institute for International Studies, 2007. http://www.diis.dk/.

Patterson, Stephen J. *The God of Jesus: The Historical Jesus and the Search for Meaning.* Harrisburg, PA: Trinity, 1998.

Plaut, W. Gunther. *Genesis: A Commentary.* The Torah: A Modern Commentary 1. New York: Union of American Hebrew Congregations, 1974.

Potsdam Institute for Climate Impact Research and Climate Analytics. *Turn Down the Heat: Why a Four Degrees Centigrade Warmer World Must Be Avoided.* A Report for the World Bank (November 2012). http://www.wds.worldbank.org/.

Rashid, Ahmed. *Descent into Chaos: The United States and the Failure of Nation Building in Pakistan, Afghanistan, and Central Asia.* New York: Viking, 2008.

———."How Obama Lost Karzai." *Foreign Policy,* March/April, 2011. http://www.foreignpolicy.com/articles/2011/how_obama_lost_karzai/.

Reeves, Eric. *A Long Day's Dying: Critical Moments in the Darfur Genocide.* Toronto: Key, 2007.

Rohrbaugh, Richard L. "A Peasant Reading of the Parable of the Talents/Pounds: A Text of Terror?" *Biblical Theology Bulletin* 23 (1993) 32–39.

Schmitt, Eric. "Pentagon Contradicts General on Iraq Occupation Forces' Size." *New York Times,* February 28, 2003. http://www.nytimes.com/2003/02/28/us/threats-responses-military-spending-pentagon-contradicts-general-iraq-occupation.html/.

Schottroff, Luise. "Human Solidarity and the Goodness of God: The Parable of the Workers in the Vineyard." In *God of the Lowly,* edited by Willy Schottroff and Wolfgang Stegemann, 129–47. Maryknoll, NY: Orbis, 1984.

Scott, Bernard Brandon. *Hear Then the Parable. A Commentary on the Parables of Jesus.* Minneapolis: Fortress, 1989.

———. "On the Road Again." *The Fourth R* 16,2 (March–April, 2003) 15.

Shapiro, Edward R., ed. *The Inner World and the Outer World: Psychoanalytic Perspectives.* New Haven: Yale University Press, 1997.

Sorkin, Andrew Ross. *Too Big to Fail: The Inside Story of How Wall Street and Washington Fought to Save the Financial System—and Themselves.* New York: Viking, 2009.

Stager, Curt. *Deep Future: The Next 100,000 Years of Life on Earth.* New York: St. Martin's, 2011.

Suskind, Ron. *The Price of Loyalty: George W. Bush, the White House, and the Education of Paul O'Neill.* New York: Simon & Schuster, 2004.

Woodward, David. *Debt, Adjustment and Poverty in Developing Countries.* Vol. 1, *National and International Dimensions of Debt and Adjustment in Developing Countries.* London: Pinter, in association with Save the Children, 1992.

Wright, N. T. *Jesus and the Victory of God.* Christian Origins and the Question of God 2. Minneapolis: Fortress, 1996.

Zaeef, Abdul Salam. *My Life with the Taliban.* New York: Columbia University Press, 2010.